DIRTY
PORTUGUESE

DIRTY PORTUGUESE

EVERYDAY SLANG FROM "WHAT'S UP?" TO "F*%# OFF!"

•••••Alice Rose, Nati Vale
& Pedro A. Cabral

Illustrated by Lindsay Mack

 Ulysses Press

Published by:
Ulysses Press
P.O. Box 3440
Berkeley, CA 94703
www.ulyssespress.com

ISBN: 978-1-56975-823-6
Library of Congress Control Number: 2010925856

Printed in Canada by Webcom

10 9 8 7 6 5 4 3 2

Acquisitions editor: Kelly Reed
Managing editor: Claire Chun
Editor: Barbara Fiori
Production: Abigail Reser
Proofreader: Lauren Harrison
Interior design: what!design @ whatweb.com
Cover design: Double R Design
Front cover photo: woman © robstyle/istockphoto.com
Back cover illustration: Lindsay Mack

Distributed by Publishers Group West

To the gente fina *in our lives who never let us forget how creative, happy and spontaneous Brazilians can be.*

TABLE OF CONTENTS

·····Acknowledgments

Alice: I would like to thank Beans for sparking my interest in Brazilian culture. Without you, I would have gone a very different path (maybe I would be eating noodles instead).

Nati: I would like to thank all those who bring out the naughty in Nati, and my parental unit for being the constant voice of reason.

Pedro: I would like to thank my parents, who tried to keep me from having a foul mouth, and my friends, who didn't let that happen.

USING THIS BOOK

We wrote this book with the assumption that you already know enough Portuguese to get by. Translation: This is not a textbook! This is a *gíria* crib sheet designed to give your Portuguese some serious street cred in Brazil. Study it carefully and use it wisely. This primer could very well help you avoid looking like an idiot. Trust us, you don't want to be the stupid *gringo* that says *obrigado* (thank you) when someone calls you a *viadinho* (gay).

Fair warning: If you quote anything from this slang book in a formal setting or with people other than your friends, no good will come from it. Learning how to use local lingo is like playing a game. So, understand the rules, learn how to follow them and then break them carefully.

This book is designed to help you save face. It is filled with up-to-date sayings: casual phrases, witty responses, sexy pick-up lines, innuendoes, etc. Each word or phrase in English is followed by its Portuguese equivalent.

One important detail you should know up front is that this book focuses only on Brazilian Portuguese because really, who wants to go to Portugal anyway?

Oh, and remember, Portuguese is NOT Spanish! Don't pretend that it is. That's just annoying.

·····Quick and dirty Portuguese pronunciation

Portuguese is pretty phonetic, so it won't take you long to pronounce unfamiliar words on your own. Here are some basics to get you started:

VOWELS

Don't be alarmed by all the accents. There are four different kinds and they always follow the same rules. Usually the second-to-last syllable in a word is automatically stressed, so when there is an acute accent (´) on a vowel, it just means the word is stressed on that syllable instead. If an acute accent is at the end of a word, it has an open sound (*café*: Ka-FÉ). The little hat, or circumflex accent (^) expresses a closed sound (*você*: vo-sÊ; like the vowel sound in "say"). A grave accent (`) doesn't change the sound of the word; it's just used for contractions. A tilde (~) makes you sound like you have a cold. It nasalizes the vowel sound (*alemã*: a-le-MÃ; like the vowel sound in "rang"). Vowels before a syllable ending with an "m" or an "n" that's followed by another consonant are also nasalized, as in the words *falam* and *quando*. Some vowels change sound when they're at the end of a word. A final position "e" (*lanche*) sounds like the "y" in baby. A final position "o" (*livro*) sounds like the "oo" in "food."

a	*parte*	like the "a" in "father"
ã	*irmã*	like the "a" in "sang"
e	*ler*	like the "e" in "bet"
ê	*português*	like the "e" in "they"
i	*comida*	like the "i" in "machine"

o	*nova*	like the "a" in "law"
ô	*avô*	like "oh"
u (stressed)	*luz*	like the "oo" in "too"
u (unstressed)	*mulher*	like the "u" in "bull"; the sound is almost nasal

CONSONANTS

Consonants are generally pronounced like they are in English, with a few exceptions. There are two consonant pairs that you will never find in English: "lh," pronounced like the "lli" in "million" (*filha*: fi-LIA; daughter) and "nh," pronounced like the "ni" in "onion" (*vinho*: vi-NiO; wine). The *c cedilla* (ç) is another distinctive consonant that is pronounced like a soft "s" where a "c" would normally represent a hard sound "k" (*coração*: ko-ra-SAO; heart).

- **c** sounds like the "s" in "sad" before "e" and "i": *cedo* (SE-du; early), *cima* (SI-ma; top). But it sounds like the "c" in "cake" before "a," "o" or "u": *cama* (KA-ma; bed), *coisa* (KOI-sa; thing), *cubrir* (KU-brir; to cover).

- **ch** sounds like the English "sh" in "shower": *achar* (a-SHAR; to think/believe).

- **d** is usually pronounced like the "g" in "gee-whiz" before "e" and "i": *saúde* (sa-U-ge; health), *dia* (GI-a; day).

- **h** is silent at the beginning of a word: *hoje* (O-je; today).

- **j** The "j" in Portuguese, like in Rio de Janeiro, is softer than it is in English, but it's not at all like it sounds in Spanish. Keep it straight.

- **l** after a vowel tends to become a "w" sound like in "few": *Brasil* (Brah-ZEW).

r at the beginning of a word and "rr" in the middle of a word are pronounced like an English "h": *Rio de Janeiro* (HI-o de ja-NEI-ro), *carro* (KA-hu; car).

s at the beginning of a word or after a consonant and a double "ss" sounds like the "s" in "seat": *sol* (SEW; sun), *conseguir* (kon-SE-gir; to obtain), *osso* (O-so; bone). But "s" sounds like the "z" in "zoo" between two vowels: *casa* (KA-za; house). In some parts of Brazil, the "s" can sound like the "sh" in "shower" at the end of a word or before "c," "f," "p," "q" or "t": *palavras* (pa-la-VRASH; words), *gostar* (gosh- TAR; to like).

t is usually pronounced like the "ch" in "cheer" before "e" and "i": *noite* (NOI-chi; night), *tio* (CHI-o; uncle).

x sounds like the "sh" in "shower" at the beginning of a word, before a consonant and sometimes before two vowels: *xarope* (sha-RO-pe; syrup). But it sounds like the "s" in "sun" between two vowels: *próximo* (PRO-si-mo; next). It can also sound like the "z" in "zoo" when "ex" is before a vowel: *exame* (e-ZA-me; test).

Nasal consonants, m and n, are pronounced through the nose, not the mouth. Hence the name.

m is nasalized when it's at the end of a syllable after a vowel, so it sounds like the "m" in "him": *combater* (kom-ba-TER; to fight). At the end of a word, "m" is barely pronounced: *sim* (yes).

n is nasalized when it comes at the end of a syllable after a vowel and before a consonant, so it sounds like the "ng" in "sing": *sensível* (seng-SI-vew; sensitive).

STRESS

Stress typically falls on the next-to-last syllable, except for words ending in "i," "u," diphthongs, consonants and nasal vowels. These words carry the stress in the last syllable. All other changes in stress require the use of a written accent, which gives a visual clue as to where to place the emphasis.

RHYTHM, CADENCE AND REGIONAL ACCENTS

Speech characteristics are determined by various factors. For example, people from different regions and socioeconomic backgrounds talk differently. One commonality, however, that is shared by most Portuguese speakers is the tendency to shorten or jam words together. This is done in different ways, from simple abbreviations (i.e., *para—pra*, *estou—tô*, *está—tá*) to more complex forms, like the use of *Ó paí ó* (Oh-pah-EE Oh) to signify *Olhe para aí* ("Oh, would you look at that."). Articulation tends to be subtle, so be careful with over-pronunciation. Americans usually sound like idiots because they try to pronounce e-ve-ry syllable. Don't be a dumb-ass, and loosen that tongue.

In this book, we've used condensed words whenever possible so that you can talk like real people do. However, keep in mind that just because something is said a certain way doesn't mean it's grammatically correct.

We've also included some indications to point out regional specific slang:

Rio de Janeiro	(RJ)
São Paulo	(SP)
Salvador da Bahia	(BA)

In conversation, people usually refer to these places as Rio, Sampa and Bahia.

Now take your *Dirty Portuguese* and get dirty with it! *Vambora* (let's go)!

CHAPTER 1

HOWDY PORTUGUESE
PORTUGUÊS CUMPRIMENTANDO

Like every other language, Portuguese has a shitload of ways to meet and greet. Asking your boss for a raise or the immigration officer to rubberstamp your passport? Keep it formal. Meeting up with your buds for a night of endless drinking or tossing a *moeda* (coin) to the neighborhood bum? No need for fancy talk.

·····Hello
Olá

When it comes to your mom and dad, don't be a snotty brat and go all casual when talking to them—show some effing respect. Same goes for anyone significantly older than you or people you meet in a semiformal situation. If you're unsure and don't want to offend someone, there's a phrase for that: *tudo bem*. Use it as a greeting and it can mean "hello," "how are you?" or even "what's up?" Use it as a response and it can mean "fine" or "it's all good."

Hello, Your Excellency Mr. President, how are you?
Olá Excelentíssimo Senhor Presidente, tudo bem?

> **I'm fine.**
> *Tudo bem.*

Hey man, what's up?
Iaí cara, tudo bem?

> **It's all good.**
> *Tudo bem.*

How are you?
Como está o/a senhor/a?

Good morning.
Bom dia.

Good afternoon.
Boa tarde.

Good evening / night.
Boa noite.

OK, done sucking up? Use these phrases with your friends or someone you just met at a party.

> **Hi.**
> *Oi.*

> **Afternoon / Evening.**
> *Boa.*

> **How are ya?**
> *Como vai você?*

> **How you doing?**
> *Como você está?*

> **What's good?**
> *Diga aí.*

> **What's new?**
> *Quais são as novidades?*

What are you up to?
O que você manda?

What's going on?
Qualé? | Kolé? (BA)
Short for *qual é.*

Whatcha up to, fool?
O que tá pegando, sacana?

What's happening, man?
Que foi, rapaz?
Literally, "What went?"

What's up, bro?
laí, bro? | laí, mano? (BA)

What's the word?
Qualé menor?

·····It's all good
Beleza

Keep your Debbie Downer comments to yourself (or save it for your stressed-out life back home). Here, it's all about the positivity. Relax, it's all good, baby!

Good.
Boa.

I'm good.
Na boa.

Okay.
Okay. (RJ) | *É nós.* (BA)

I can't complain.
Só alegria.
Literally, "only happiness."

Everything's...
Tudo...

> **all right.**
> *certo.*
>
> **joyful.**
> *jóia.*
>
> **at peace.**
> *em paz.*
>
> **in order.**
> *em ordem.*
>
> **cool.**
> *legal.*
>
> **beautiful.**
> *beleza.*
>
> **good.**
> *na boa.*

·····How you doing?
Como você tá?

What are you doing?
O que você tá fazendo?

What's going down?
O que tá rolando?

What's good?
Qual é a boa?

Whatcha got?
O que tá pegando?

What's going on?
O que você manda?

·····It's been ages
Tem muito tempo

Long time no see.
Tem uma cara que não te vejo.

It's been a while since I've seen you.
Tem uma pá de tempo que não te vejo.

Where've you been?!
Cadê você?! (BA)
Literally, "Where are you?"

You've been M.I.A.!
Você sumiu!
Literally, "You disappeared."

You've grown a goatee since I last saw you.
Na última vez que eu te vi, você não tinha essa barbicha.

·····Sorry
Desculpa

You never know who you're gonna offend, so it's always nice to be prepared with these save-your-ass favorites.

Pardon.
Perdão.

A thousand apologies.
Mil desculpas.

I'm really sorry. (like when you're actually sympathetic to the person)
Sinto muito.

Excuse me.
Com licença.

Scuse me.
Licença.

Exsqueeze me.
Licença aí. (BA)

Sorry about that, brah.
Desculpa aí, meu broder.

Excuse my shitty accent.
Me desculpe pelo meu sotaque carregado.

My bad.
Foi mal.

Woopsy daisy.
Foi mal por essa cagada.
Literally, "It was bad, this poop."

That was all my fault.
A culpa foi toda minha.

I screwed up.
Vacilei.

I fucked up.
Dei mole.

·····Please and thank you
Por favor e obrigado

Americans have a bad rep for being arrogant and rude. Shocking, huh? If you don't wanna come off as a complete prick, memorize some of these:

Please.
Por favor.

Pleez.
Na manha. (BA)

Pretty pleez.
Por favorzinho. (RJ) | *Na moral.* (BA)

Do me a favor.
Me faz um favor. (RJ) | *Faça o favor.* (SP)

Thank you.
Obrigado/a.

Thanks.
Brigado/a.

Thanks a bundle.
Muito obrigado/a.

Thanks so much for doing me that favor.
Muito agradecido pelo favor que você fez.

Thanks a lot.
Valeu.

I owe you one.
Quando você casar a/o mulher/marido é toda/o sua/seu.
Literally, "When you're married, I'll never try to go after your wife/
husband."

You're welcome.
De nada.

No problem.
É nenhuma. (BA)

Don't be ridiculous.
Imagina.

·····Introducing yourself
Se apresentando

Hi, my name is Chad.
Oi meu nome é Chad.

I'm American.
Sou americano.

I've just arrived in town.
Cheguei agora.

Where's the nearest beach?
Onde fica a praia mais próxima?

I heard that Copacabana has a tsunami of asses.
Ouví dizer que Copacabana tem um tsunami de bundas.

I'm Greta.
Meu nome é Greta.

I'm from Germany.
Sou da Alemanha.

Do you know a good youth hostel nearby?
Você sabe onde tem um albergue perto daqui?

Is it OK if I go topless here?
Posso fazer topless aqui?
FYI: Local Brazilian women do not go topless and you shouldn't either. On the other hand, a little ass-cheek never hurt anyone.

·····Nice to meet you
Prazer em conhecer você

Pleasure.
Prazer.

Glad to meet you.
Muito prazer.

It was a pleasure.
Foi um prazer.

The pleasure is mine.
O prazer é todo meu.

Likewise.
Igualmente.

What do you do to kill time?
O que você faz pra matar o tempo?

What do you do with your free time?
O que você faz no seu tempo livre?

What do you do?
O que você faz da vida?

Where do you live?
Onde você mora?

KISSES)))
BEIJOS

People get friendly when it comes to greetings. It's a little peck on each cheek if you're friends, and if it's between two guys, usually a casual hand bump or maybe a manly hug. Also, and this is mostly on the phone, you send a kiss before you hang up.

Bye girl, kiss.
Tchau menina, beijo.

Kiss.
Beijo.

Another.
Outro.
This can be a response to *beijo.*

Send a kiss to your mom.
Manda um beijo pra sua mãe.

Big kiss.
Beijão.

Little kiss.
Beijinho.

Smooches.
Beijocas.

Do you live alone?
Você mora sozinho/a?

Can I use your bathroom?
Posso usar seu banheiro?

Have you ever had an STD?
Você já teve algum tipo de DST?
DST is short for *Doença Sexualmente Transmissível.*

Can you help me find a hot girlfriend?
Você pode me ajudar a arrumar uma namorada gostosa?

Gotta light?
Você tem isqueiro?

Where's the best pick-up soccer game around here?
Onde posso bater uma pelada?

••••Good-bye
Adeus

Bye.
Tchau.

Bye-bye.
Tchauzinho.

See ya.
Até.

Later.
Até já.

See you next time.
Até a próxima.

See you later.
Até mais.

See you soon.
Até logo.

See you whenever.
Até qualquer hora.

••••I'm going
Já vou

'Cuz sometimes you've just gotta make like a tree and leave.

I'm gone.
Fui.

I'm out.
Vou abrir o gás. (BA)

It's about friggin' time.
Já vai tarde.

I'm gonna split like a banana.
Vou meter o pé. (RJ)

I gotta run.
Vou partir a mil.

I'm gonna leave.
Vou embora.

It's time to go.
Tá na hora.

I'm...
Tô...

> **outta here.**
> *caindo fora.*
>
> **leaving.**
> *saindo.*
>
> **bouncing.**
> *vazando.*
>
> **outtie.**
> *indo.*

Stop by anytime.
Apareça.

Stop by more often.
Apareça mais.

Come back soon.
Volte logo.

Come back anytime.
Volte sempre.

Peace out.
Fica na paz.
Literally, "Stay in peace."

Peace.
Axé. (BA)
Literally, "Good energy."

·····Amen to that!
Amem!

Brazil is a Catholic country, and though a lot of people don't go to church, a lot do. So even when you're having one last drink for the road or leaving a *samba* club after a raucous night of partying, your farewells may sound like Sunday High Mass at Igreja da Penha. Even if you aren't part of the flock, the proper response for these phrases is *Amem* (we promise you won't go to hell, you unbeliever).

Go with God.
Vai com Deus.

Stay with God.
Fica com Deus.

Stay in the faith.
Fica na fé.

God bless you.
Deus te abençoe.

God be with you.
Deus te leve.

May God bless you.
Que Deus te abençoe. (RJ) | *Meu pai Oxalá te abençoe.* (BA)
Jesus Christ is represented by a god named Oxalá, one of the many *orixás* (gods and goddesses) in Candomblé, an Afro-Brazilian polytheistic religion.

Go with God.
Fé em Deus.
Literally, "faith in God."

May God watch over you.
Que Deus te proteja.

CHAPTER 2

FRIENDLY PORTUGUESE
PORTUGUÊS AMIGÁVEL

Fala sério! (You're kidding!) Brazilians are friendly and talkative and like to joke around and kick it most of the time. Laid back and liberal, they don't take themselves or others too seriously. Teasing is second nature to almost everyone. So, when you're out and about, just relax and don't take anything too personally. For the most part, it's all about having fun.

·····Friends
Amigos

Chances are you're not going to become anyone's BFF if you're just in Brazil on vacation. But who's stopping you from trying? Brazilians use many terms to describe their range of friends based on affection.

> **How's it hangin', guys?**
> *Tudo bem **pessoal**?*
>
> **I'm going out with my crew tonight.**
> *Hoje vou sair com a **galera**.*
>
> **Whassup, peeps!**
> *Oi, **gente**!*

Yo, homey!
*Iaí **amigão**!*

Homeboy
Parceiro

Boy (like a close friend, not a child)
Camarada

> **He's my boy.**
> *Ele é meu **camarada**.*

Good guy
Gente boa

Dude
Cara (RJ) | *Bicho* (BA)

> **What's up dude? You ain't gonna believe this.**
> *Iaí **bicho**? Você não vai acreditar nisso.*

Man
Rapaz | *Rapá* (SP)

> **What's going on, man?**
> *Qualé **rapá**?*

Brother
Irmão

> **It's all good, my brother.**
> *Tudo beleza meu **irmão**.*

Dogg
Fiel

> **Leave him alone, he's my dogg.**
> *Não mexe com ele, o cara é meu **fiel**.*

Bro
Bro | *Mano* | *Meu* (SP)

> **Bro, you have to come with us.**
> ***Mano**, você tem que vir com a gente.*

Buddy
Bródi

Brah
Broder
Yep, that's right. It's the Brazilian brother from another mother.

> **'Sup, brah?**
> *Fala, **broder**?*

Fag
Boiola
Can be used in a friendly way or as an insult.

> **Fuck you, fag!**
> *Vai tomar no cú, **boiola**!*

Faggot
Viado
Just like *boiola*, *viado* can be friendly or seriously insulting.

> **How you doing, faggot?**
> *Iaí **viado**, tranquilo?*

Sis
Mana

> **I love that girl. She's like a sis to me.**
> *Eu adoro essa menina. Ela é como se fosse minha **mana**.*

Colleague
Colega

> **I can't stand my work colleagues.**
> *Não aguento meus **colegas** de trabalho.*

Boy / Girl
Menino/a

> **Where've you been, girl?**
> *Por onde você andava, **menina**?*

Boyfriend / Girlfriend
Namorado/a

> **No, I don't have a boyfriend.**
> *Não, eu não tenho **namorado**.*

Date
Paquera

> **Laura's date is hot.**
> *O **paquera** da Laura é gostoso.*

····Personal traits
Características pessoais

Wow! Considering how ugly you are, your sister's a total babe.
*Nossa! Considerando o quanto você é feio, sua irmã é uma **gata**.*

Your classmate's such a fox. Do you think she'll go out with me?
*Sua colega é uma **tigresa**! Você acha que ela vai ficar comigo?*

Nobody likes a drama queen.
*Ninguém gosta de uma **rainha do drama**.* (RJ)

You're a…
Você é um…

Stop being a…
Deixa de ser…

> **dork.**
> *babaca.*
>
> **kiss-ass.**
> *puxa-saco.*
>
> **dick.**
> *otário.*
>
> **fuck-up.**
> *vacilão.*
>
> **fucker.**
> *sacana.*
> Sacana can also be translated as "fool," like something you would call your friend. It's all about context.

····Family
Família

This may come as a shock to you, but most Brazilians happily live at home well into their 20s.

Mother
Mãe

Mom
Mãezinha (RJ) | *Mainha* (BA)

Mommy
Mamãe

Father
Pai

Dad
Papai

Daddy
Paizinho

Grandfather / Grandmother
Avô / Avó

Grandpa / Grandma
Vovô / Vovó

Cousin
Primo/a

Uncle / Aunt
Tio/a
This is also an affectionate term for any older friend, even if you're not blood related.

·····Everyday people
Gente do dia a dia

Stereotypes exist for a reason, and they're usually based on reality. You may not like it. You may not give a shit. But there's no way around them. Might as well know what they are.

Caipira: Hillbilly.

Fanfarrão: Big mouth.

Galinha: Player (a guy) or slut (a girl)…that's just the way it is in the Latin American world of machismo. Literally, "chicken."

Malandro: A scoundrel; also called *pilantra*.

Maria Chuteira: A woman who dates soccer players. *Chuteira* means "cleats."

Maria Gasolina: A woman who dates guys with fancy cars. *Gasolina* means "gas."

Maria Tatami: A woman who's notorious for dating *jiu-jitsu* players. (*Tatami* refers to the mats they use in *jiu-jitsu*.)

Moleque: A young boy. This can also refer to a boy who's a brat.

Nerd: No explanation needed. Same word, same meaning.

Mauricinho (male) / *Patricinha* (female): Socialite, trust-fund baby.

Playboy: A wannabe *mauricinho* who is mainly a womanizer.

Perua: A hella flashy woman (often used when describing older women, but not always). Literally, "turkey."

Piriguete: A hoochie.

•••••Characters
Personagens

Tired of the PC bullshit all over the U.S.? Well, you'll love Brazil, where everyone tells it like it is, even if it hurts. You better be proud of who you are 'cuz you're certainly gonna hear about it—good or bad. Here are a few nicknames based on personality, looks and nationality.

You're a(n)...
Você é um/a...

    tattletale.
    dedo-duro.

    gossip.
    fofoqueiro/a.

    thug.
    pilantra.

    bum.
    vagabundo/a.

    hustler.
    vigarista.

    rascal.
    pivete.
    Also another term for "homey" (*amigão*).

    ugly woman.
    canhão.

    snoop.
    xereta.

    idiot.
    trouxa.

    slut.
    piranha.

clingy person.
carrapato. | papel de bala. (RJ)
Carrapato means "tick," while *papel de bala* is "candy wrapper."

whore.
vagabunda.

loser.
zero à esquerda.

Joe Schmoe.
Zé Ninguém.

You're...
Você é...

    easy.
    piriguete.

    shameless.
    cara de pau.
    Literally, "wooden face."

    stingy.
    pão duro.
    Careful how you say this. *Pão* means "bread" but *pau* means "dick." *Pão duro* is literally, "hard bread," while *pau duro* is a "hard on."

    old-fashioned.
    careta.

hard-headed. (in the dumb sort of way)
cabeça-dura.

crazy.
maluco.

·····Between you and me
Cá entre nós

Let's be honest, sometimes less is more. Use these to keep the conversation going without actually listening.

Uh-huh.
Hurum.

Oh-oh.
Chiii.

Oh, no!
Ai ai ai!

Exactly.
Isso.

Absolutely.
Com certeza.

Agreed.
Falou.

What do you mean?
Como assim?

Got it.
Tô ligado.

For real?
É mesmo?

Beats me.
Sei lá.

So what?
E daí?

RACE)))
RAÇA

Brazil is a melting pot of Native Brazilians, Portuguese, Africans, Japanese, Germans and Italians. With centuries of intermixing, race just isn't that big a deal, so there's a lot of racial labeling that isn't necessarily insulting.

Black
Nego/a
While *negro* (black) may read as "negro," an outdated term your mama's mama used back in the day, it's perfectly acceptable. The more casual *nego* is popular with close friends; it's like a term of endearment—whether you're dark or not. *Preto*, on the other hand, is not a word to utter lightly—it can be highly offensive. To be safe, don't use it unless you're black (or looking for a smack down).

White
Parmalat
Parmalat is a brand of milk.

Native American
Índio
Yeah the whole "looking for India, found a new world instead" thing is part of South America, too.

Asian
Japa
Because practically every Asian in Brazil is Japanese.

Arab
Turco

Anyone else who isn't Brazilian
Gringo

I don't care.
E eu com isso?

Never mind.
Deixa pra lá.

Are you serious?
Tá falando sério?

Seriously?
Jura?

I can't believe it.
Não acredito.

That's bullshit.
Que besteira.

Wow!
Nossa! (RJ) | *Vixi!* (BA)
Short for *Nossa Senhora*—the Virgin Mary.

What!
Oxente! (BA)

Gosh!
Puxa!

Damn!
Droga!

It happens.
Faz parte.

Make do.
Se vira.

Whatever.
Tanto faz.

It's no use.
Não adianta.

I don't give a shit.
Não tô nem aí.

·····Terms of endearment
Palavras de carinho

Brazilians are a touchy-feely bunch. They're all about creating intimacy. An easy way to do that is by using diminutives, which are generally formed by adding the suffixes *-inho* and *-inha* to nouns, adjectives and names. So the phrase, "Mom can you make some treats for me to take to the party" (*Mãe pode preparar uns salgados pra a festa?*), would turn into something ridiculous like, "Mommy, could you make some little treaties for my little party?" (*Mainha, pode preparar uns salgadinhos pra minha festinha?*) In English it sounds like sucking up, but in Portuguese it's normal.

Augmentatives can also express intimacy, but an indication of respect is thrown in the mix. For example, the movie *The Godfather* is known in Brazil as *O Poderoso Chefão*, which literally means "The Powerful Big Boss."

Darling
Querido

Sweetheart
Coração

Pumpkin
Meu bem
Literally, "my welfare."

Cutie
Fofo/a

My love
Meu amor

Honey
Docinho (RJ) | *Meu/minha nego/a* (BA)
Meu nego/minha nega literally means "my black boy/girl."

Sweetie
Meu filho/minha filha
Literally, "my son/daughter." But the phrases are commonly used to address close friends, or between people with a high degree of intimacy.

·····Sweet talkin'
Falar doce

If you're gonna go through the awkward steps of dating, at least try to know what you're talking about.

HUGS AND KiSSes)))
ABRAÇOS E BEIJOS

Although you probably aren't going to say any of these words out loud, it's nice to know for recounting your date to your friends the next day.

Carinho: Physical affection

Cócegas: Tickle

Cafuné: Caress someone's head gently

Selinho: Soft kiss

Chupão: Strong kiss (like a plunger)

Dar uns Amassos (RJ): Heavy petting

To flirt
Flertar

To be a flirt
Dar mole

> **She's a flirt!**
> *Ela dá mole pros caras!*

To hit on
Dar em cima de alguém

To pick someone up
Pegar alguém

To mac on someone
Azarar alguém

Player
Pica de mel

Pimp
Farpado
Literally, "barbed-wire fence."

Can I have your number?
Me dá seu telefone?

Have we met before?
A gente já se conhece?

You look really pretty tonight.
Você tá linda hoje.

Can I buy you a drink?
Quer beber alguma coisa?
Literally, "Do you want to drink something?" but it's implied that he's gonna pay.

Wanna dance?
Quer dançar?

We danced together at the party all night long!
Dançamos juntos a festa toda!

Can I kiss you?
Posso beijar você?

Do you wanna go out with me?
Quer ficar comigo?

Where to?
Onde a gente vai?

Let's…
Vamos…

> **take a walk.**
> *dar um rolé.*

> **go to the movies.**
> *ao cinema.*

> **go back to my place.**
> *pra minha casa.*

I want to spend the night with you tonight.
Quero dormir com você hoje.

I went on a date with him last night.
Tive um encontro com ele ontem à noite.

CHAPTER 3

PARTY PORTUGUESE
PORTUGUÊS DE FESTA

Ain't no lie, Brazilians know how to party. Hell, the whole country screeches to a halt every year for Carnaval, a month's worth of nonstop mayhem. Maybe it's the blazing sun, the gorgeous people or the ridiculous number of holidays... whatever the reason, in Brazil, anything goes when it comes to having fun.

·····Let's go out
Vamos sair

Brazilians are kinda flaky about making plans; they looooove keeping their options open. Just because someone agrees to do something in advance, it doesn't mean it's actually going to happen. The good news is it's a two-way street—you can bail, too, without seeming like a jerk.

It's going down tonight.
Vai rolar hoje à noite.

It's gonna happen.
Vai acontecer.

You in?
Você topa?

I'm in.
Topo.

I'm out.
Tô fora.

Wanna go?
Você quer ir?

Yeah!
Quero!
Questions are rarely answered with *sim* or *não*. Use the present tense of the verb instead.

Sure!
Claro!

Of course!
Claro que sim!

Count me in!
Tô nessa! | Tô dentro! (RJ)

Nah, I don't feel like it.
Não, num tô a fim.
Num is short for *não estou*, which sounds like "num" when said together quickly.

Next time. I'm feeling lazy today.
Fica pra próxima. Tô com preguiça hoje.

So, is that a yes?
Então, aceita meu convite?

> **Yep.**
> *Aceito.*

> **I already said yes.**
> *Já aceitei.*

> **Maybe.**
> *Pode ser.*

Let me think about it.
Deixa eu ver.

I don't think so.
Acho que não.

Nope. But have fun!
Não obrigado/a. Mas divirta-se!

Are you coming?
Você tá vindo?

Relax, I'll be there.
Relaxa, eu estarei lá.

Are you gonna show up to my birthday party?
Você vai aparecer na minha festa de aniversário?

Take it easy, I'll show up.
Fica tranqüilo que eu vou aparecer.

I'll make an appearance.
Vou dar uma chegada.

Come!
Vem!

Come over!
Chega aqui!

Get over here!
Vem cá!

You're late!
Demorou!

Hurry up!
Depressa!

Move it!
Não demora!

Man, it's been three hours—she stood you up.
Rapaz, já passaram umas três horas—acho que ela te deu um bolo.

HE SAID, SHE SAID)))
ELE FALOU, ELA FALOU

Gringas get hit on, *gringos* get rejected. Sorry guys, that's just the way it is.

THE BRAZILIAN GUY SAYS:

Hello beautiful.
Oi linda.

You're hot.
Você é gostosa.

Do you come here often?
Você vem sempre aqui?

You want to hook up?
Quer ficar comigo?

THE BRAZILIAN GIRL SAYS:

That creep keeps looking over here.
Aquele cara esquisito fica olhando pra cá.

I think he has a crush on me.
Acho que ele tá na minha.

He's definitely into me.
Ele tá a fim de mim.

Stop trying to get with me!
Para de me azarar!

Party's over, bro.
A festa acabou, bro.

It's done.
Já era.

Let's bounce.
Bora.

Let's go home.
Vamos pra casa.

Go away!
Vai embora!

Get out of here!
Sai daqui!

Leave!
Sai fora!

Get lost!
Cai fora!

Did you have fun?
Você curtiu?

I had a blast.
Curti de montão. | *Curti à vera.* (RJ)

I had a great time.
Me diverti muito.

It was great.
Foi ótimo.

It was cool.
Foi legal. | *Foi maneiro.* (RJ) | *Foi bacana.* (SP) |
Foi massa. (BA)

It was awesome.
Foi show de bola.
Literally, "It was a ball show."

•••••Chillin'
Na boa

It's not really about where you go, but who you're there with.
Of course, some places are more exciting than others.

Let's…
Vamos…

visit.
*fazer uma **visita**.*

stop by.
*fazer uma **visitinha**.*

drop by.
*dar uma **passada**.*

go for a ride.
dar uma volta.

catch a flick.
assistir um filme.

throw a party.
dar uma festa.

have a BBQ.
*fazer um **churrasco**.*

have a kick-it.
*fazer uma **festinha**.*

go clubbing.
*pra **balada**.*

Invite everyone.
Chama geral.

·····At the beach
Na praia

Ipanema, Copacabana…some of the best beaches in the world are in Brazil. But don't expect a visit to be a solo venture of thoughtful introspection. The sands are packed with bodies preening, sunning, playing volleyball, selling food, hawking trinkets—it's got all the serenity of Grand Central Station at rush hour.

Let's go for a dip.
*Vamos dar **um mergulho**.*

I don't want to swim now.
*Num tô a fim de **nadar** agora.*

I just want to…
Só quero…

> **sunbathe.**
> *tomar sol.*

get some color.
pegar uma cor.

get a tan.
pegar um bronze.

Can you put some sunscreen on my back?
*Passa **protetor** na minhas costas?*

Take it easy on the rays—your skin looks like beef jerky.
Cuidado com o sol—sua pele tá parecendo um maracujá.
Maracujá means "passion fruit," which has a shriveled rind.

That Speedo makes your balls look huge.
*Essa **sunga** deixa suas bolas enormes.*

Who's that chick with that bangin' bod?
*Quem é aquela gata com aquele **corpaço**? (RJ)*

Your bikini's rad—where'd you get it?
*Seu **biquíni** tá bem legal—onde você comprou?*

Where's the nearest beach bar?
*Onde fica a **barraca** mais próxima?*

Nice tan line!
*Que **marca/marquinha** linda!*
This is not sarcastic. In Brazil, the bigger and darker the tan
line, the better. If you don't believe us, grab a Brazilian *Playboy*
magazine and see for yourself.

Where's that guy selling the sarongs?
*Onde tá aquele cara vendendo as **cangas**?*
Don't even think about bringing a big ol' towel to the beach.
A sarong will do just fine.

·····Vendors
Vendedores

Let's not pretend that you aren't visiting the touristy places.
Even if you don't want to buy anything, just lying on the beach
puts you in the target zone. You're a tourist and you stand out
like a tourist, so the locals are gonna try to rip you off. Don't let
anyone put a necklace on you or tie anything to your wrist—it's
a pain trying to politely tell someone that you don't want his
crappy jewelry. And please don't let that big "sucker" tattooed
across your forehead prevent you from getting a fair deal. If
you do actually want to make a purchase, here are some good
phrases to know.

How much is this?
Quanto é?

How much does this cost?
Quanto custa?

How much is it for a dozen bananas?
Quanto é a dúzia de bananas?

Can I have it for less?
Pode fazer mais barato?

Come on man, I'm a local.
*Vem cá rapá, eu **sou da terra**.*
Literally, "I'm from the land."

I'm from around here.
Eu sou daqui. (RJ)

That's crazy expensive.
Tá caro pra caramba. (RJ) | *Tá caro como a porra.* (BA)

How much will you give it to me for?
Por quanto você faz?

Can't you give me a better price?
Pode fazer mais barato pra mim?

A piece of shit like this?
Uma porra dessa?

You're totally ripping me off.
Aí você me fode.

Son of a bitch, that's fucking expensive!!
Puta que pariu, tá caro pra caralho!!

Go fuck yourself, I'm outta here.
Vai se fuder, vai morrer burro.
Literally, "Go fuck yourself, you're going to die a donkey." These are strong words, so say it like you mean it and then bail.

·····Carnival
Carnaval

Carnaval is the biggest, baddest party on the planet. To experience it is to know what it means to be Brazilian: happy, fun, uninhibited, smoking hot and sexy. We could start by explaining that Carnaval has European origins and coincides with the conclusion of the Roman Catholic Lent blah blah blah … but let's skip to what you actually want to know—what city to visit during the week-long debauchery.

Brazil has many types of Carnaval with regional differences in music, dance and food. In our opinion, the top three party-central choices are Rio, Recife and Salvador.

RIO DE JANEIRO

Rio de Janeiro is the Carnaval the world knows: a parade of elaborately costumed men and women dancing *samba*. The official parade isn't free (and is actually in a large open-air exhibition space called the Sambódromo, not the city streets)—so you'll pay some green to sit in the bleachers. But there are also free street parties, with their own samba music, everywhere.

This Carnaval, I'm gonna watch everything from the bleachers.
*Nesse Carnaval vou assistir tudo da **arquibancada**.*

I want to go to a Carnaval party.
*Quero ir a um **baile de Carnaval**.*
Baile de carnaval is a pre-Carnaval party at a club. This is only at Rio's Carnaval.

Where is the samba school rehearsal?
*Onde tem ensaio de **escola de samba**?*
There are about a dozen Rio samba schools that labor year round to create floats and costumes, compose music and lyrics, and choreograph really amazing dance performances for Carnaval. Each school has an hour to parade down the street with their music.

Mangueira's parade was spectacular.
*O **desfile** da Mangueira foi um espetáculo.*
Mangueira is one of Rio's samba schools.

Where can I buy parade tickets?
*Onde compro os **ingressos** para o desfile?*
What? Did you think it was free to watch?

What are the lyrics to this samba enredo?
*Qual é a letra desse **samba enredo**?*
Each samba school composes a new song every year that'll loop over and over again during their hour-long performance; these thematic songs are called samba *enredo*.

I loved the **Front Commission** of this samba school.
*Adorei a **comissão de frente** dessa escola de samba.*
The *comissão de frente* is a group of about a dozen people who
lead off their samba school's parade. The group usually wears
very elaborate costumes that represent the samba school's
annual theme (e.g., secrets, magic, etc.).

RECIFE

In Recife, the official Carnaval music is *frevo*, not samba. The
rhythm is fast paced and difficult to dance to, so good luck
learning it—maybe after a few *latões* (tall ones) you'll catch on.
Or not. There's also an official parade, plus plenty of private
celebrations.

What costume are you gonna wear?
*Qual vai ser a sua **fantasia**?*
Unlike in Rio, you don't need to be part of a samba school to be
in the Carnaval parade.

What time does Rooster of the Morning start?
*Que horas começa o **Galo da Madrugada**?*
Galo da madrugada is the biggest Recife *bloco*, a group of people
who are associated with a particular float in the parade.

Who's gonna perform on this stage tonight?
*Quem vai tocar nesse **palco** hoje?*

I want to learn how to dance *frevo*.
*Quero aprender a dançar **frevo**.*

SALVADOR

In Salvador, *axé* music runs the party. It's six days of nonstop revelry in the streets with music blaring Salvador's favorite singers and bands atop grand floats. People pay to walk and dance along with the float, and everyone wears a T-shirt representing what *bloco* (group) they are in. They're not playing around. Salvador's Carnaval is in the *Guiness Book of World Records* as the biggest street party in the world—probably because every year there's an average of 2 million people celebrating Carnaval here.

Did you see Carlinhos Brown's float this year? It was awesome!
*Voce viu o **trio elétrico** do Carlinhos Brown esse ano? Foi massa!*
Trio elétrico is an electric float that the singers and bands ride on through the streets.

Where do I buy a T-shirt for Daniela Mercury's group?
*Onde compro a camiseta do **bloco** da Daniela Mercury?*
The *bloco* includes the *trio elétrico* and the group of people surrounding it. It is blocked off from the rest of the people by a big rope.

I'm broke, this year I'm just going to be in the crowd.
*Tô duro, esse ano vou ficar na **pipoca**.*
Pipoca (literally, "popcorn") are the people on the other side of the rope (i.e., those not part of a *bloco*). While they can't walk next to a float, they can jump around to any and all of the groups (like popcorn). Be careful here because there are a lot of thefts and fights that occur.

I'm tired of getting my ass grabbed. Let's go to a club tomorrow night.
*Estou cansada de ter minha bunda apertada, vamos pra um **camorote** amanhã.*

For the people who don't wanna be squeezed in with a million people on the street, they can watch from above in clubs built just for Carnaval (then taken down at the end of the week). We're not saying they aren't crowded, too, but it's a little better.

·····Boozing
Embebedando-se

At one point or another, you're bound to get drunk. If you're lucky though, it might just loosen your tongue.

Let's get a drink.
*Vamos tomar um uma **birita**.* (RJ) | *... **uma**.* (SP) | *...**copo**.* (BA)

Nightclub
Boate

Danilo says he hates nightclubs because they're too loud. Yeah right! It's because he has two left feet.
*Danilo diz que detesta as **boates** porque tem barulho demais. Mentira! É porque ele tem dois pés esquerdos.*

We're going to a cool little bar. You wanna come?
A gente vai pra um barzinho bem legal. Você quer vir?

Blowout
Farra

Bender
Bebedeira

Binge
Encher a cara

Cheers!
Saúde!

HOLIDAYS AND FESTIVALS)))
FERIADOS E FESTIVAIS

If you want to see how Brazilians really get down, plan your trip to coincide with a holiday or festival. Oh, wait, there's an official festivity practically every week of the year. In fact, we doubt there's any other country in the world that has as many days off as Brazil does. Not only do you take off a week for Carnaval and a crapload of religious holidays, but during the World Cup when the *Seleção Brasileira* plays, everyone gets time off to watch the game and no one has to go to school. And when Brazil wins the World Cup, the next day is automatically a holiday. Now, why are you living in America? Here are a few of the big holidays:

January 1: *Ano novo/Réveillon* (New Year's Day).

2nd Thursday in January: *Lavagem do Bonfim* (BA)—A parade that ends at a famous church in Salvador where you get to wash the church steps (ain't piety great?).

February/March: *Carnaval*—Depending on where you are, the festivities go on for two to six days, and if you can handle it, a few days more.

March/April: *Páscoa* (Easter)—The whole nine yards: Good Friday (*Sexta-feira Santa*), Hallelujah Saturday (*Sábado de Aleluia*) and Easter Sunday (*Domingo de Páscoa*).

June: *Festas Juninas*—A collection of June holidays that celebrate various Catholic saints—*Santo Antonio* (St. Anthony), *São Pedro* (St. Peter) and *São João* (St. John). In some northeast states, the parties last for an entire month.

July 2: *Dia de Independência* (BA)—Independence Day. This is the day when the last Portuguese left Brazil.

September 7: *Dia de Independência*—Independence Day. The day that Emperor Don Pedro I declared Brazil an independent country (although there were still some Portuguese occupying certain states, hence the July 2 festivities when the last damn Portuguese actually left).

December 25: *Natal* (Christmas).

One more!
Mais uma!

He's going to get drunk at his bachelor party tonight.
Ele vai ficar bêbado na despedida de solteiro dele.

Get someone else drunk
Embebedar alguém

Every time Gonçalo drinks, he gets hammered and ends up making a fool of himself.
*Toda vez que o Gonçalo bebe, ele acaba perdendo a linha e **pagando mico**.*
Literally, "paying a little monkey."

I'm...
Tô...

> **tipsy.**
> *de pileque.*

> **drunk.**
> *bêbado.*

> **wasted.**
> *travado.*

> **smashed.**
> *bebum.*

> **loaded.**
> *embriagado.*

> **woozy.**
> *tonto.*

·····Types of drunks
Tipos de bêbados

Realization #1: Drunkenness is universal. Realization #2: There is never just one kind of drunk.

> **Sleepy drunk**
> *O bebo-bosta*

> **Touchy-feely drunk**
> *O sensível*

> **Funny drunk**
> *O palhaço*

> **Quiet drunk**
> *O altista*

Friendly drunk
O amistoso

Happy drunk
O alegre

Angry drunk
O valentão

The drunk who thinks he's the shit
O fodão

Neanderthal drunk
O bêbado Neanderthal
The drunk that can't speak in complete sentences and grunts a lot.

Mr. "It's time to bring up old shit that you've done"
O lavador de roupa suja
Literally, "the dirty clothes washer." So much for forgive and forget. This drunk just can't seem to give it a rest. Like the saying goes: *in vino veritas*.

Mrs. "I'm so fat, aren't I?"
Senhorita "ohh, eu sou tão gorda"
When she's drunk, her insecurities are magnified.

·····Booze
Birita

Beer-lovers rejoice—the foamy drink is by far the beverage of choice, followed by *caipirinhas*, mixed drinks made with *cachaça* (a liquor similar to rum), sugar and lime. Brews are ordered by the bottle (*garrafa*) and drunk from mini glass cups (*copinhos*), except at the beach or in the street, where you can buy it by the can. Draft beer is not served in pints, but don't freak out, the *chopp* (draft beer) will keep coming and coming and coming until you decide you're done. So, down the hatch!

I want…
Eu quero…

a drink.
um goró.

a *cachaça*.
uma cachaça.
Brazil's version of rum, this spirit is made from fermented sugarcane juice. It's most commonly drunk in a fruity concoction, but you can also find the good stuff, spiced with different herbs, and drink it straight. This drink is everywhere (it's also known as *pinga* and *aguardente*).

a *caipirinha*.
uma caipirinha.
Brazilians fucking love this cocktail made of *cachaça*, sugar, crushed limes and ice.

a *caipiroska*.
uma caipiroska.
Cocktail made of vodka, sugar, fruit of choice (strawberries, limes, kiwi…) and ice.

a glass of wine.
um copo de vinho.
You can get red (*tinto*) or white (*branco*), but try to go for the Argentinean or Chilean brands because the Brazilian wine is as sweet as Manischewitz.

a chaser.
uma bebida fraca.

a shot.
uma dose.

brandy.
conhaque.

rum.
rum.

whiskey.
uísque.

vodka.
vodka.

tequila.
tequila.

liquor.
licor.

champagne.
champanhe.

cider.
sidra.

beer.
cerveja.

> **Can I get an ice-cold beer?**
> *Me traz uma **cerveja** bem gelada?*

a brewski.
uma cerva.

a brew.
uma creva.

> **I'm going to grab a ridiculously cold brew.**
> *Eu vou pegar uma **cerva** estupidamente gelada.*

suds.
uma brisa.

an ale.
um gel.

a draft.
um chopp.

a cold one.
uma gelada.

a pale ale.
uma lora.
Short for *loira*, which means "blond."

•••••The morning after
Na manhã seguinte

Every action has a reaction. Consider yourself warned.

> **I feel awful.**
> *Me sinto péssimol.*

> **I'm...**
> *Tô...*

> > **hungover.**
> > *de ressaca.*

sick.
doente.

nauseous.
enjoado.

going to throw up.
com vontade de vomitar.

I drank too much *cachaça* and woke up hurling.
*Bebi cachaça demais e acordei **chamando o Raul**.*
Literally, "I woke up calling out to Raul"—because the name Raul
sounds like the sound you make when you throw up.

I feel like shit.
Tô me sentindo uma merda.

I have the spins.
Minha cabeça tá rodando.

I'm going to pass out.
*Vou **desmair**.*

I'm never drinking again.
Não vou beber nunca mais.
Yeah, like you're not gonna use this sentence.

I puked on your couch.
***Vomitei** no seu sofá.*

·····Weed
Maconha

Weed is probably the most popular drug in Brazil. You can buy it almost anywhere, though you might need to search a little to find the good stuff. Possession is illegal, so be cautious of where you choose to light up.

Roach
Bagana

Bud
Bagulho

Pot
Barro

Bomb
Bomba

Gray
Cinza

Devil's herb
Erva do diabo

Peace herb
Erva da paz

Chalk
Giz

Pink mango
Manga rosa

Grass
Mato seco

Ganja
Tora

A joint (*fininho*) is:

a doobie
uma marola

a cricket leg
uma perna de grilo

a doob
um baseado

a jay
um brau

a long neck
um beck

a fattie
uma vela

The act of smoking weed (*fumar maconha*) is:

give a deuce
dar dois

slap a panther
um tapa na pantera

slap a monkey
um tapa na macaca

burn coal
brazar

grill coconut
chapar coco

fill the mouth
encher a boca

pull a crazy
puxar um doido

pull a long neck
puxar um beck

Can I light up here?
Posso fumar aqui?

Let's get high.
Vamos fazer a cabeça.

Do you want to buy some herb?
Você quer comprar um pouco de erva?

Do you know where can I score an ounce?
Você sabe onde posso arrumar um peso?

> **Ask Carlos, he's a stoner.**
> *Pergunta pro Carlos, ele é chincheiro.*

> **Or try Maria. Let's be honest, she's also a pothead.**
> *Ou pergunta pra Maria. Falando sério, ela também é maconheira.*

> **You gotta go to a drug corner.**
> *Você tem que ir na boca.*

·····Cocaine
Cocaína

Cocaine is cheap and plentiful in Brazil, and like weed, there's a lot of different names for it.

> **Blow**
> *Brizola*

> **Powder**
> *Pó*

> **Dust**
> *Poeira*

> **Yayo**
> *Rapa*

> **Nose candy**
> *Papelote*

White
Branca

Flour
Farinha

I wanna…
Eu quero…

> **sniff some blow.**
> *cafungar uma brizola.*

> **snort yayo.**
> *cheirar rapa.*

> **powder my nose.**
> *meter a napa no pó.*

Marcelo likes to snort snow.
*Marcelo gosta de **cheirar pó**.*

Forget it, he's too amped up.
Deixa pra lá, ele tá ligadão.

I've never smoked crack.
*Nunca fumei **crack**.*

Daniel's a crackhead—he loves rock.
*Daniel é **pedreiro**—adora **pedra**.*

I don't want you turning into a crackface.
*Não quero que você vire um **sacizeiro**.*

·····Cops
A polícia

Police can get a bit rough if you're up in their face, and even if you're not. It would be wise not to provoke them. Just saying…

> **Watch out for the cops!**
> *Cuidado com a **polícia**!*

> **Keep your eyes open!**
> *Fica de olho!*

Pay attention!
Se liga!

Stay frosty!
Fica esperto!
Literally, "Stay sharp."

Fuck! Here comes the po again.
*Porra! Aí vem a **patrulinha** de novo.* | *...**bolinha**...* (RJ)

That cop car has been posted here every day.
*Aquele **camburão** tá parado aqui todos os dias.*

Group of cops
Patamo (RJ)

Psst, there is a pig over there.
*Psiu, tem um **cana** lá.*

That MP was super intimidating.
*Aquele **PM** foi muito intimidador.*
The military police (*polícia militar*) are the city beat cops, so you'll
see them everywhere and most often. The city cops (*polícia civil*)
function more like detectives who investigate local crimes. And
the federal police (*polícia federal*) are just like the U.S. feds—
they fight bigger stuff like drug cartel crimes and governmental
corruption.

CHAPTER 4

BODY PORTUGUESE
PORTUGUÊS CORPORAL

•••••Looking good
Tá bonito

In Brazil, it's all about appearances—unlike here in the States (right). The better you look, the easier your life will be. For girls it's about thick legs and a tight ass. For guys it's big biceps and a chiseled six-pack. And whether you're at the gym, the beach or the office, there's never a no-make-up-and-ratty-sweats day. You take care of your body and dress well because other people notice and will judge. (But not you, of course. No, you would never judge. Never.)

He/she is...
Ele/ela é...

handsome/pretty.
bonito/a.

beautiful.
lindo/a.

sexy.
sexy.

cute.
bonitinho/a.
Can also be used for someone who is ugly but dresses well.

adorable.
fofo/a.

gorgeous.
lindíssimo/a.

hot.
gostoso/a.

attractive.
atraente.

stylish.
estiloso/a.

She's got a bangin' body.
*Ela tem um **corpaço**.* (RJ) | *...**corpo massa**.* (BA)

He's really built.
*Ele é **malhado**.*

I love men when they're cut.
*Adoro homens **sarados**.*

This girl is a fine piece of meat.
*Essa mulher é **um filé**.* (RJ)

Your brother's a stud.
*Seu irmão é **um gato**.*

He looks like he's on 'roids. He's a beast!
*Parece que ele toma **bomba**. Tá parecendo um **búfalo**!*

Damn, she's a 10.
Puxa, ela é um pitel. (RJ)
Pitel is a girl who is fine, smells good and dresses well.

Your boyfriend's got it going on.
Seu namorado é um pão. (RJ)
Pão (bread) is the male version of *pitel*.

I'm only into girls with good figures.
*Só gosto de mulheres que tem **shape legal**.*

She's got a nice body.
*Ela tem um **corpo maneiro**.* (RJ)

You've got beautiful eyes.
*Você tem um **belo par de olhos**.*

Your beefy lips would make Angelina Jolie jealous.
*Sua **boca carnuda** faria Angelina Jolie ficar com inveja.*

Her butt is so perky I could sit on it.
*O bumbum dela é tão **empinado** que eu poderia sentar nele.*

Careful with those rock-hard boobs—I don't want to scratch my eye out.
*Cuidado com esse **peito duro**—não quero furar meus olhos.*

Are those fake boobs? Can I touch them?
*Você tem **silicone no peito**? Posso pegar?*

Dude, your mom's a total MILF.
*Cara, sua mãe é uma **coroa gostosa**. | ... **coroa enchuta**.* (BA)

I'd like to wash my underwear on his washboard.
*Queria lavar minhas calcinhas nesse **tanquinho**.*

Your wife's got dope legs.
*Sua mulher é **pernuda**.*

He thinks he's all that.
Ele se acha o tal.

He's struttin' his stuff with that six-pack.
*Ele **tá tirando onda** com o **abdomen sarado** dele.*

·····Ugly
Feio

On the other hand, if you happen to be funny-looking or have inherited some unfortunate family traits, don't count on polite silence on the subject. Oh, you're going to hear about it.

He/she is...
Ele / ela é...

>> **ugly.**
>> *feio/a.*

>> **pretty ugly.**
>> *bem feinho/a.*

>> **really ugly.**
>> *feião/feiona.*

>> **fucking ugly.**
>> *feio/a pra caralho.*

>> **fugly.**
>> *feio/a que nem a porra.* (RJ) | *feio/a pra porra.* (BA)

>> **cross-eyed.**
>> *vesgo/a.* (RJ, SP) | *zarolho/a.* (BA)

>> **hairy.**
>> *peludo/a.*

>> **thin.**
>> *magro/a.*

>> **skinny.**
>> *magrelo/a.*

>> **scrawny.**
>> *seco/a.*

>> **chubby.**
>> *gordinho/a.*

>> **chunky.**
>> *balofo/a.*

Dude, your cousin is heinous.
*Cara, sua prima é **uma baranga**.* (RJ)

YOU BETTER SHAPE UP)))
FICA NA LINHA

Unlike in the Western world, where a shade above anorexic is sexy, Brazilians have a healthier body image. Curves, muscles, ass—let's get some meat on those bones. Skinny ain't sexy here.

She looks like **Olive Oyl**.
Ela parece a Olivia Palito.

He's fucking **frail**.
Ele tá seco pra caralho.
Literally, "dry" (like a leaf).

She's definitly **anorexic**.
Pode acreditar, ela tá anorexica.

You're **rail thin**!
Você tá chupada viu!
Literally, "sucked."

What happened? You're super skinny.
O que aconteceu? Você tá na capa do Batman.
Literally, "on Batman's cape."

Your sister's a **mess.**
*Sua irmã tá um **bagaço**!*

He's as **fat as a whale**.
*Ele é **gordo que nem uma baleia**.*

I was born with a **double chin** and it never
went away.
*Nasci com essa **papada enorme** e nunca saiu.*

I don't have a **beer gut**—it's a glandular problem.
*Eu não sou **barrigudo/a**—tenho um problema glandular.*

Check out that **bug-eyed midget.**
*Olha aquele anão com **olho de boi**.*
This is also a term for someone who wants everything you have.

He / She has...
Ele / Ela tem um/uma...

a melon head.
cabeção.

a big mouth.
bocão.

Dumbo ears.
orelhão de Dumbo.

a huge nose.
narigão.

four eyes.
quatro olhos.

a belly.
banha na barriga.

clown feet.
pezão.

·····Nicknames
Apelidos

Brazilians like to give people nicknames. If your name is long, it's shortened; if it's short, it's shortened even more. But you can only hope for a variation of what's on your birth certificate. More likely than not, your Brazilian friend will zero in on the one thing you spent years in therapy for...and the next thing you know, everyone's calling you *Pouca telha* (Turtle waxer).

Shorty
Baixinho/a

Baldy
Careca

Turtle waxer
Pouca telha
Literally, "little roof."

Egghead
Cabeça de ovo

Buck-toothed
Dentuço/a

Pinhead
Cabeça de pica (BA)

Metal mouth
Boca de lata

> **Hey, metal mouth!**
> *Iaí, **boca de lata**!*

Pinocchio
Pinóquio

Oxygen thief
Ladrão de oxigênio

Dwarf
Anão

Bottle cap (small person)
Tampinha

> **Who does this bottle cap think he is?**
> *Quem esse **tampinha** pensa que é?*

Little one
Pequeno/a

Toothpick
Palito

> **Can you lift this barbell, toothpick? Or will your arms snap in two?**
> *Você pode levantar essa barra, **palito**? Ou seus braços vão quebrar.*

Skeleton
Carcaça

> **Go out with that skeleton? No way!**
> *Namorar com aquela **carcaça**! Nem pensar!*

Fatty
Bola sete

> **What do you want, fatty?**
> *O que você quer, **bola sete**?*

Tall man
Poste (like a lamppost)

Giraffe
Girafa

Big guy
Montanha

Giant
Grandão

Juicer
Sabirila

> **Your brother is such a juicer.**
> *Seu irmão é um **sabirila**.*
> Sabirila is short for *perna de sabiá e corpo de gorila*, or "bird legs and gorilla body."

Ugly man
Barango (BA)

This bitch thinks she's the shit, doesn't she?
Esse trubufu se acha né?

·····Piss and shit
Mijar e cagar

For some reason poop and pee aren't that funny in Brazil. That doesn't mean *you* don't find them funny.

> **I need to…**
> *Preciso…*
>
>> **urinate.**
>> *urinar.*
>>
>> **go pee.**
>> *fazer xixi.*
>>
>>> **Can I go pee here? I'm about to burst.**
>>> *Posso **fazer xixi** aqui? Tô apertado.*

go pee-pee.
fazer pipi.

go number 1.
fazer o número 1.

> **You're gonna go number 1, right?**
> *Você vai **fazer o número 1**, né?*

take a piss.
mijar.

take a leak.
tirar água do joelho.
Literally, "take water out of the knee."

defecate.
defecar.

go poop.
fazer cocô.

go number 2.
fazer número 2.

take a dump.
cagar.

take a shit.
bater um cagão.

let the mud slide.
largar o barro.

I have to piss like a fucking racehorse.
Tô morrendo de vontade de mijar.

My dick is full of piss.
Meu pau está cheio de mijo. (BA)

I'm constipated.
Estou com prisão de ventre.
Literally, "prison of the womb."

That *vatapá* gave me diarrhea.
*Aquele vatapá me deu **diarréia**.*

Somebody's got the shits!
*Alguém tá com **caganeira**!*

I laughed so hard **I wet myself**.
*Me **mijei** de rir.*

Your boxers are nasty man, they always have **skid marks**.
*Tenho nojo das suas cuecas, sempre estão **freiadas**.* (BA)

·····Other bodily functions
Outras funções corporais

I'm gassy.
Estou com gases.

I can **burp** the alphabet, you wanna hear?
*Eu posso **arrotar** o alfabeto, você quer ouvir?*

We farted at the same time, that must mean something!
***Peidamos** ao mesmo tempo, deve ser um sinal!*

Uhhh, you **ripped one**!
*Hmmm, você **soltou um pum**!*

Who **cut the cheese**?
*Quem **soltou uma bufa**?*

That waiter **spat** in your juice.
*O garçom **cuspiu** no seu suco.*

Don't **blow your nose** on my shirt.
*Não **assoa o nariz** na minha camisa.*

Is that **snot** on your cheek?
*Isso é **catarro** na sua bochecha?*

What's up with your son? He's always eating his **boogers**.
*Que porra é essa? Seu filho sempre tá comendo **meleca**.*

Does your dog have fleas? **I'm itching** like crazy!
*Seu cachorro tem pulgas? **Tô me coçando** que nem a porra!*

Your breath is worse everyday, fool!
*Seu **bafo** tá cada dia pior, sacana!*

French people never shower. They always have the worst B.O.
*Os franceses nunca tomam banho. Sempre tão com **C.C.***
We're gonna go out on a limb and guess that C.C. means *cheiro do corpo* (body odor).

·····Menstruation
Menstruacão

In Brazil there doesn't seem to be any problem with sharing information about Aunt Flo. Guys can call girls out on PMS, and girls tell guys about how heavy their flow is. So don't be alarmed if you hear a little TMI.

I'm on my period.
*Tô no **vermelho**.*

Careful, it's that time of the month.
*Cuidado, ela tá **naqueles dias**.*

Honey, I can't tonight, I'm on the rag.
*Docinho, hoje não posso porque **tenho visita**.*

I'm gonna get pussy! Yeah right. She must be riding the crimson tide.
*Que bocetão nada, deve **tá de boi**.*

I have cramps.
*Tô com **cólica**.*

Are you PMSing?
*Tá de **TPM**?*

Can you pick up some pads at the store before you go out with the guys?
*Você pode comprar **absorvente** no supermercado antes de sair com seus amigos?*

·····I'm sick
Tô doente

Oh man, I don't feel so good.
Cara, não tô me sentindo muito bem.

What's wrong with you?
O que você tem?

I feel like crap.
Tô mal.

My ass is sore.
Minha bunda tá doendo.

Man, I have a killer headache!
Cara, essa dor de cabeça tá me matando!

I have...
Estou...

> **a fever.**
> *com febre.*
>
> **a sore throat.**
> *com dor de garganta.*
>
> **a cough.**
> *tocindo.*
>
> **a runny nose.**
> *com o nariz escorrendo.*
>
> **a stuffy nose.**
> *com o nariz entupido.*
>
> **a stomachache.**
> *com dor de barriga.*
>
> **swine flu.**
> *com Gripe Suína.*

It sounds like you have a cold.
*Parece que você tá **resfriado/a**.*

For Brazilians, tea (*chá*) is medicine. Whatever the problem, there's a tea for it—from the common cold to a sore throat to an abortion.

Do you have tea for nausea?
Você tem chá pra azia?

Tea for... *Chá pra...*	Name *Nome*	Description *Descrição*
headache	*camomila*	chamomile
stomachache	*boldo do chile*	a leaf from an evergreen shrub
sore throat	*gengibre*	ginger
cough	*jiló*	scarlet eggplant (this tea is gargled rather than drunk)
common cold	*alho*	garlic
fever	*folha de pitanga*	leaves from the Brazilian cherry tree (*pitanga*)
gas	*erva doce*	anise leaf
kidney stone	*quebra-pedra*	stonebreaker herb
weight loss	*picão preto*	Spanish needle, a rainforest herb
abortion		this you'll have to look for on your own...

If chamomile tea just ain't doing it, here are some useful words:

I need...

    medicine.
    remédio.

    aspirin.
    aspirina.

    ibuprofen.
    Anador. (brand name)

    muscle relaxant.
    relaxante muscular.
    Look for it under the brand name Dorflex.

cough medicine.
xarope.

allergy medicine.
anti-alérgico.

zinc lozenges.
pastilhas.

laxative.
laxante.

Neosporin.
cicatrizante.

CHAPTER 5

HORNY PORTUGUESE
PORTUGUÊS FOGOSO

Teeny bikinis, sexy dancing and a mountain of porn—if you can't get some action in Brazil, you're probably not trying. That said, this is a Pope-loving country, so don't expect the chase to be easy (you know, the whole Catholic-waiting thing). Once you've scored your hottie, you'll need to take her back to your place or a motel because chances are she still lives with her parents and her dad might kill your *gringo* ass if he finds you in bed with his princess. But when you're finally behind closed doors, feel free to try out some sweet talking.

•••••Fucking
Fodendo

I wanna…
Quero…

Let's…
Vamos…

> **go back to my place.**
> *pra minha casa.*

have sex.
transar.

do it.
fazer sexo.

make love.
fazer amor.

make whoopie.
fazer um tchuco. (BA)

have a quickie.
dar uma rapidinha.

go to a motel and fuck.
pro motel foder.

fuck like animals.
trepar como animais.

ride the bony pony.
meter a vara. (BA)
Literally, "dip the stick."

Today, there's no way out of it, I'm gonna **lay my pipe**.
*Hoje não tem jeito vou **afogar o ganso**.*
Literally, "drown the goose."

I don't wanna go out with her, I just wanna **break her off** and I'll be good.
*Não quero namorar com ela, só quero **molhar o biscoito** e tá bom.*
Literally, "wet the cookie."

You don't even know how bad I wanna **bone** her.
*Você nem imagina o quanto eu quero **trepar** com ela.*
Trepar literally means, "to climb."

Clara's mom is a MILF—I'd like to **hit that**.
*A mãe de Clara é uma coroa gostosa—queria **comer ela**.*

Do you wanna **hook up**?
*Você quer **ficar** comigo?*

MOTELS)))
MOTEIS

In Brazil, a motel isn't an affordable lodging choice; it's explicitly designed as a rendevous point for one-night stands and booty calls. It's that pesky living-at-home situation—how can you get busy if your parents are eating dinner in the next room? Thus the birth of the love motel to *dar uma* (get'r done). If you're unsure of where to go, look for the Vegas-style, 24/7 neon lights. Rooms rent by the hour, and standard units come with with mirrored ceilings and walls, a set of extra sheets and, as if you're not horny enough, a TV full of free porn. You can get fancier rooms (with an erotic chair or a jacuzzi bathtub), but you'll pay more. Forgot your edible panties or condoms? Don't worry, you can buy it at the motel, along with other well-chosen items.

Room service
Serviço de quarto

Can you bring up some fresh **sheets**? Ours have blood stains.
Você pode me trazer lençóis limpos? Esses tão sujos de sangue.

Should we do it in the **shower**?
Vamos transar no chuveiro?

How much is it **per hour**? I've got a lot of energy tonight.
Quanto é por hora, tô com muita energia hoje?

I'd like a room with the **erotic chair**.
Quero um quarto com cadeira erótica.

Does the medieval suite come with chain-mail armor?
A suíte medieval vem com armadura?
Some motels have themed rooms: Egyptian, Japanese, Western—you get the idea.

I don't wanna makeout too much, let's get straight to **doin' the nasty.**
*Não quero muito beijo na boca, vamos direto pro **rala e rola**.* (RJ)

It's time to get freaky, my little flower.
Tá na hora do vamos ver, minha florzinha. (RJ)

·····Cocks
Rolas

Most guys are uncut, because of the Catholic background and all, so don't be surprised when their banana still has the peel.

Suck my...
Chupa meu/minha...

Grab my...
Segura meu/minha...

penis.
pênis

dick.
pau.

You may also hear "Bráulio" used for the word "dick." This common Brazilian name gained national prominence as a synonym for "dick" in 1995. What happened? The Ministry of Health adopted "Bráulio" as a nickname for "penis" in a commercial for AIDS awareness. In true capitalistic style, the ad campaign flooded the airwaves with mentions of "Bráulios," cementing the name's infamous association with the penis. A number of people who were actually named Bráulio sued the company because of the forever-lasting connection with the male member. Now it's against the law to use the name "Bráulio" in commercials about sex or AIDS.

pole.
pica.

ding-dong.
longue-dongue. (BA)

wang.
cacete.
Literally, "roll of bread."

little wiener.
bimba.

thing.
caralho.

worm.
minhoca.

wiener.
pinto.
Literally, "chick."

sword.
espada.

weenie.
pipí.

banana.
banana.

lollipop.
pirulito.

tripod.
tripé.

elephant trunk.
tromba.

sausage.
lingüiça.

big snake.
anaconda.

baseball bat.
bastão.

clapper. (the dangling part of a bell)
badalo.

·····Blow jobs
Boquetes

Like in English, there's an endless list of words and phrases for a BJ. We're just skimming the surface here.

Blowey
Chupeta
Literally, "pacifier."

Bola-gato

A homonym for the English words "ball" and "cat," which said in a Brazilian accent sounds like *boquete*, which means "blow job."

I'd like to **deepthroat** this!

*Queria **cair de boca** nisso!*
Cair de boca literally means "to fall onto (with an open mouth)."

Your sister **gave me a hummer** last night.

*Sua irmã **cantou no meu microfone** ontem a noite.*
Cantar no microfone literally means "sing into the microphone."

To suck dick

Chupar manga
Literally, "to suck a mango."

To give head

Tocar uma flauta
Literally, "to play the flute."

·····Pussy
Buceta

Lick my...

Chupa meu/minha...

Touch my...

Toca meu/minha...

vagina.
vagina.

goods.
abará. (BA)
Abará is a starchy steamed street treat that's split open and filled with "the goods," one might say. It's kind of like a *tamale*, but the dough, made from black eyed peas, is mixed with dried shrimp and spices.

coochie.
xereca.

cooch.
piriquita.

cunt.
perereca.
Literally, "female toad."

twat.
xoxota.

bearded clam.
bacalhau.
Literally, "salted codfish."

piss-meat.
carne-mijada.

persued pussy.
perseguida.

beaver.
tabaco.

pooch.
testa.

clitoris.
clitóris.

button.
botão.

bean.
broto de feijão.

cashew.
castanha.

garlic clove.
dente-de-alho.

clit.
pinguelo.

pencil eraser.
dedo sem unha.
Literally, "finger without a nail."

·····Ass
Bunda

Brazilians are all about the ass. So here are some ways for you to make the ass your biggest ass-et.

Slap my…
Bate no/a meu/minha…

Squeeze my…
Aperta meu/minha…

Put your finger in my…
Coloca seu dedo no/na meu/minha…

buttocks.
glúteos.

little butt.
popozinho.

big butt.
popozão.

bum.
bumbum.

ass.
bunda.

booty.
traseiro.

flat ass.
bunda de aspirina.
Literally, "aspirin ass."

fat ass.
bunda de melancia.
Literally, "watermelon ass."

little booty.
bunda de acarajé. (BA)
Acarajé is a small snack you can buy on the street.

Anus
Cú

Tail
Rabo

Badunkadunk
Cadeiras

Junk in the trunk
Balaio (BA)
Balaio is the big basket people carry on their heads.

•••••Tits
Tetas

Lick my…
Chupa meu/minha…

Grab my…
Segura meu/minha…

boobs.
peitos.

hooters.
air bags.
Don't forget the Brazilian accent—*air bagis*.

melons.
melões.

suckers.
chupetas.
Literally, "pacifiers."

headlights.
comissão de frente.
Literally, "first to arrive." In Rio's Carnaval, the parades are divided into sections. The first part is the *comissão de frente*, and it's usually the part that draws the most attention.

knockers.
seios.

mammaries.
mamas.

ugly boobs.
peitolas.

perky breasts.
peito empinado. (RJ) | *peito duro.* (BA)

Put on a bra—I can't stand looking at your saggy boobs.
*Coloca um sutiã, num guento mais ver esse seu **peito de lama decendo a ladeira**.*
Literally, "mud sliding down a hill."

She's so flat-chested, you can't even suck her tits.
*Não da pra chupar aquele peito de **ovo frito**.*
Literally, "fried egg."

·····Balls
Bolas

I fucked so much that my balls are empty.
*Fudi tanto que minhas **bolas** estão vazias.*

Slide your tongue between my nuts.
*Passa língua entre os meus **ovos**.*

I like to feel your ball sack hitting my ass.
*Gosto de sentir seu **saco** batendo na minha bunda.*

Why does your **scrotum** have so much skin on it? You could make a tambourine out of it.
*Por que tem tanta pele no seu **escroto**? Dá pra fazer um tamborim.*

I shaved my **nads**, don't they look bigger?
*Raspei meus **culhões**, não parecem maiores?*

Eww, your **jewels** are shriveled.
*Eca, seus **bagos** tão murchos.*
Literally, "a cluster of fruits" (like grapes).

·····Getting in the sack
Entrando na cama

Portuguese is a romance language, so even if you're saying "Suck it harder, bitch," as long as you whisper it lovingly, it'll sound like angels are speaking.

I want you all to myself tonight.
Quero você só pra mim hoje.

You turn me on.
Você me dá muito tesão.

When you kiss me like that it gives me a hard-on.
Quando você me beija assim meu pau fica duro.

Tell me how you like it.
Me fala como você gosta.

Get undressed and lay down.
Tira a sua roupa e deita.

I'm very excited.
Estou muito exitado/a.

Grab my cock.
Segura o meu pau. (RJ) | ...a minha rola. (BA)

Your cock is huge!
Seu pau é enorme! (RJ) (SP) | Sua rola é muito grande! (BA)

Put it in your mouth.
Coloca na sua boca.

Like this?
Assim?

Give me a blow job.
Faz um boquete.

It's so hard!
Tá tão duro!

Suck it slower/faster.
Chupa devagar/mais rápido.

Are you wet?
Tá molhadinha?

Do you want me to finger you?
Quer uma siririca?

Do you like it?
Você gosta?

It feels so good.
Tá gostoso.

Lick my balls.
Chupa as minhas bolas.

Swallow everything!
Engole tudo!

You shaved!
Tá raspado!

Sit on my dick.
Senta no meu pau.

Move around a little.
Mexe, rebola.

Don't stop.
Não pare.

Are you cumming?
Tá gozando?

I'm gonna cum!
Vou gozar!

I want to cum in your mouth.
Quero gozar na sua boca.

Was it good for you?
Foi bom pra você?
If you're going to ask this, you better be ready for the answer.

·····Sexual acts and perversions
Atos sexuais e perversões

Missionary is sex 101. If you want to get past the beginner's seminar, read on.

I want to do it…
Quero fazer um…

> **missionary style.**
> *papai-mamãe.*
> With legs spread, it's called *frango assado* (roast chicken).

> **doggy-style.**
> *de quatro.*

Do you like… ?
Você gosta… ?

Wanna try… ?
Quer experimentar… ?

> **69**
> *meia-nove*

> **finger banging**
> *siririca*

> **oral sex**
> *sexo oral*

> **the wheelbarrow**
> *carrinho de mão*

the one-legged kangaroo
canguru perneta

cowgirl
coqueirinho

the reverse cowgirl
escorpião

titty fucking
espanhola

a threesome
sexo a três

an orgy
uma orgia

group sex
uma suruba

anal sex
sexo anal

I'm tired of...
Estou cansado/a de...

cuddling.
ficar aconchegado.

kissing.
beijar.

foreplay.
preliminares.

dry humping.
me esfregar.

eating pussy.
beijar a perereca.
Literally, "kiss a female toad."

·····Going down
Chupada

I think if I **eat you out** you'll be happy.
*Acho que **uma linguadinha** vai deixar você mais feliz.*

Could it be that today you're finally going to **munch her carpet**?
*Será que hoje finalmente você vai **cair de boca no tapete**?*

Don't be shy, I'm going for a **muff dive**.
*Deixa de timidez, quero **lavar o carro por baixo**.*
Literally, "wash a car upside down."

·····Masturbation
Masturbação

Let's face it, everybody does a little solo work from time to time.

Jack off
Tocar uma bronha

Whack off
Descascar uma

5 against 1
5 contra 1

Stroke the salami
Acariciar o salame

Scalp the clown
Descabelar o palhaço

Roll the dice
Jogar dados

I usually get off with a vibrator, but a dildo will do it in a pinch.
*Quase sempre gozo com um **vibrador**, mas um **dildo** vai quebrar o galho.*

Do you have any porn with grannies in it?
*Você tem filme **pornô** com mulheres velhas?*

·····Contraceptives and pregnancy
Contracepção e gravidez

Do you have a… ?
Você tem um/uma… ?

Shit, the…broke!
Merda, o/a…estourou!

> **condom**
> *camisinha*
>
> **rubber**
> *capacete*
>
> **raincoat**
> *capote*
> Literally, "sweatshirt."
>
> **beenie**
> *touca*
>
> **Johnny hat**
> *chapéu*

You can keep going, I'm on the pill.
*Pode continuar, eu tomo **pílula**.*

I'm late.
Minha menstruacão tá atrasada.

I'm pregnant.
Tô grávida.

Preggers
Buchuda (BA)

Knocked up
Embuchada (BA)

This is my baby mama.
Essa é a mãe do meu filho.

·····Gays and lesbians
Gays e lésbicas

Brazil is a free country when it comes to expressing yourself. It welcomes gays, lesbians and certainly trannies. It's something about the nice weather and cute clothes that just make everyone let go and embrace their inner woman or man.

Tranny
Traveco

Homo
Baitola

Queer
Bicha

Girl (in a gay sort of way)
Biba

She-male
Mulher-com-pau
Literally, "woman with a dick."

Doll
Boneca

Fruit
Frutinha
This is used for the young who aren't sure they're gay (but everyone else knows they are).

Pillowcase biter
Mastiga fronha

Fag
Boiola | Baitola (BA)

Faggot
Viado

Lesbian
Lésbica

Lesbo
Sapatona

Dyke
Sapatão

Butch
Maria / João

CHAPTER 6

ANGRY PORTUGUESE
PORTUGUÊS ZANGADO

Brazilians don't have self-esteem issues—they're proud to be Brazilian, they're proud to be frickin' beautiful and they're proud of kicking the world's ass in soccer. So watch what you say about things the locals hold sacred. Declaring that the country's soccer team is a bunch of washed-up has-beens may be a bad idea—Brazilians are the world's best fighters and the last thing you want is some big-'roided jiu-jitsu master pounding your ass.

·····Enemies
Inimigos

Hopefully you won't make any enemies while you're in Brazil, but that doesn't mean you can't complain about the ones back home. Oh, and not to offend anyone from Deutschland, but a common synonym for "enemy" in Brazil is *alemão* (German). Hmm, guess *someone* did something fucked up in this part of the world, too.

Ex
Ex-namorado/a

Landlord
Proprietário

Boss
Chefe

Cops
Os homi
Short for *homens* (men).

Pigs
Os canas

5-O
Os gambés

Stepmother
Madrasta

Stepfather
Padrasto

Politician
Político

Mother-in-law
Sogra

Father-in-law
Sogro

Hustler
Um-Sete-Um
Literally, "171," refering to article 171 from the Brazilian Penal Code that basically says it's a crime to take advantage of someone in a way that leaves them at a loss or injured.

Thief
Ladrão

Rapist
Estuprador

Lawyer
Advogado

Pervert
Tarado

·····Talkin' shit
Falando mal

She always making a **tempest in a teapot.**
*Ela sempre faz uma **tempestade num copo d'água**.*

Those bitches are such **gossips.**
*Aquelas putas são tão **fofoqueiras**.*

That was a **low blow.**
*Foi um **golpe baixo**.*

He totally **put ideas in my head.**
*Ele **botou minhoca na minha cabeça**.*
Literally, "put worms in my head."

My ex-wife is always **getting in the way.**
*Minha ex-mulher é **uma pedra no meu sapato**.*
Literally, "a rock in my shoe."

I can't stand that asshole.
__Num guento__ mais aquele cuzão.

You guys are always **bickering**.
Vocês duas sempre tão __batendo boca__.

Goiânia is **the pits**.
Goiânia é a __treva__.

SpongeBob totally **annoys me**.
Bob Esponja enche __meu saco__.

He's way too **hardcore** for me.
Ele __é hardcore__ demais pra mim.

You think you're ripped? Your arms look like
broomsticks.
Você acha que tá malhado? Você tem braço de vassoura.

I'll get them back, just you wait.
Eu vou dar o troco, pode esperar.

Look at her, she's so embarrassed. She left with her
tail between her legs.
*Olha ela, ficou com vergonha. Meteu o rabo entre as
pernas e saiu.*

He totally had me **against the wall**.
Ele realmente me __deixou de saia justa__.

My brother always **picks on me**.
Meu irmão sempre __pega no meu pé__.

You really **screwed up** this time.
__Meteu os pés pelos mãos__ dessa vez.
Literally, "to put your feet where your hands go."

Don't worry, she always **gives in**.
Num esquenta, ela sempre __topa__.

Are you trying to fool me again?
Tá me enrolando de novo?

SWEARING)))
CHINGANDO

Swear words have been around since the grunt of the Neanderthals, so in Brazil it's no different—there's a ton of ways to express your frustration.

Darn!
Caramba!

Shoot!
Miséria!

Shucks!
Diabo!

Cunt!
Buceta!

Disgrace! (believe us, this is a lot stronger in Portuguese)
Desgraça!

Shit!
Merda!

Fuck!
Caralho!

And then there's *porra*. The word *porra* is like a call girl—it can be anything you want it to be. It can be an exclamation like "dammit," "shit" or "fuck." Or, in attempt to be as confusing as possible, the word can be used as an emphasis, an adverb, a noun or even a comma.

Dammit!
Porra!

What the **fuck** are you doing here?
Que porra você tá fazendo aqui?

What the **hell** is this?
Que porra é essa?

She's **fucking** ugly.
Ela é feia que nem a porra.

It's **hella** far.
Longe como a porra.

I don't like this **shit**.
Não gosto dessa porra.

The name's Bond, James Bond.
Meu nome é Bond porra James Bond.

·····Insults
Insultos

Liar
Mentiroso/a

Bastard
Safado/a

Slut
Galinha

Skank
Cachorro/a
Literally, "dog."

Whore
Vagabundo/a

Ho-bag
Ordinário/a

Douchbag
Descarado/a | *Pela saco* (RJ)

Some gems to use with your ex-girlfriend:

Heifer
Vaca

Gold digger
Pistoleira

Hoochie
Periguete

Bitch
Puta

And a few to hurl at your ex-boyfriend:

Dick
Otário

Dumbass
Mané

Tard
Retardado

Imbecile
Imbecil

Idiot
Idiota

Doofus
Comédia

Fuck-up
Vacilão

Asshole
Cuzão

·····You talkin' to me?
Tá falando comigo?

It's all in the tone. Some of these phrases aren't really fighting words unless you say them with an ugly glare and harsh tone.

What?
Qualé?

Wassup?
Qual foi?

Is there a problem?
Algum problema?

What do you want?
Qual é mesmo?

What are you looking at, fuck-up?
O que você tá olhando, vacilão?

What the fuck are you looking at?
Que porra você tá me olhando?

Do you like dick or something? Why are you looking at me?
Tô com cara de pica? Tá me olhando por que?

Are you a faggot?
Você é viado?

Do you not see me, motherfucker?
Não tá me vendo filho da puta?

Is your eye in your asshole?
Tá com o olho no cú?

·····Get outta my face!
Sai da minha frente!

Stay away from me!
Fica longe de mim!

Leave me alone.
Me deixa em paz.

Get off it!
Larga do meu pé!

Move it, fatso.
Sai daqui, gordo/a.

Go away!
Sai pra lá!

Outta my business.
Vai procurar o que fazer.

Get to steppin'.
Vaza mané.

Beat it, dick.
Mete o pé, otário. (RJ)

I don't want to see your ugly mug again.
Não quero te ver nem pintado de ouro.
Literally, "I don't want to see you even if you are painted with gold."

Go to hell!
Vai pro inferno! (RJ) | *Vai pra porra!* (BA)

Take your hands off me!
Tira sua mão de mim!

Get lost, you creep.
Vai ver se eu tô na esquina.
Literally, "Go see if I'm around the corner."

Screw you!
Vai se danar!

Go back to the bitch that made you!
Vai pra puta que pariu!

Up yours!
Vai tomar no cú!

Piss off!
Vai se ferrar!

Fuck off!
Vai se lenhar!

Go fuck yourself!
Vai se fuder!

•••••Shut up!
Cala a boca!

Shut your piehole!
Fecha essa boca!

Shut your trap!
Fecha o bico!

I don't wanna talk about it!
Nem vem que não tem!

Quit sayin' that!
Vira essa boca pra lá!

You talk a lot a bullshit.
Você só fala merda.

Dude, you gotta take it seriously!
Cara, tem que levar a sério!

What he says doesn't mean shit.
O que ele fala não se escreve.

Don't be such a negative Nelly.
Deixe de ser espírito de porco.

When you're quiet, you're a poet.
Você calado é um poeta.

Take that engagement ring and shove it up your ass!
Pega sua aliança e enfia no cú!

•••••Fightin' words
Palvaras de briga

If you wanna hit a guy where it hurts, just question his manly manliness. But you better know who the fuck you're about to throw down with—there are a lot of baaaad people in Brazil who make the Mob look like Archie and the gang.

Even my 90-year-old grandmother punches harder than you.
Até a minha avó de noventa anos tem um soco mais forte que o seu.

Say that one more time if you have the guts.
Repita isso se você for homem.

I'll fuck your team up.
Eu vou fuder o seu time.

Let's fight man to man.
Vamos brigar mano a mano.

Shit's about to go down!
O coro vai comer! (RJ)

You're gonna lose, motherfucker!
Vai acabar dançando, filho da puta!

Better stop pushing me, I don't wanna have to get rough with you.
Melhor parar de me empurrar, não quero ter que bater em você.

I'm gonna kick your ass.
Eu vou surrar você.

Come on you faggot, I'm gonna destroy you.
Vem viado, vou te quebrar todo.

Did you just bitchslap that blind guy?
*Você acabou de **dar um tapa** naquele cara cego?*

I'm gonna break your face in half.
Eu vou partir a sua cara no meio.

They fucked shit up last night.
Eles quebraram o pau ontem á noite.

She punched me in the balls, dude.
*Ela **deu um soco** nas minhas bolas, cara.*

Punch him in the jaw like you mean it!
***Dá um murro** no queixo dele com vontade!*

Kick him in the head. Oops, I think he's dead.
***Chuta** a cabeça dele. Ops, acho que ele morreu.*

I'll give you a dollar if you go pinch that midget's ass.
*Te dou um dólar se você **beliscar** a bunda daquele anão.*

Your cousin got knocked out last night.
*Seu primo levou um **nocaute** ontem á noite.*
Nocaute is pronounced *knock-outy*.

That dyke gave me a black eye.
*Aquela sapatona me deixou de **olho roxo**.*

I'm going to headbutt that *flanelinha* if he get's near my car.
*Vou dar uma **cabeçada** naquele flanelinha se ele chegar perto do meu carro.*
Flanelinhas are on every street corner in Brazil. They wait around to "help" you park your car. And even if they don't help, they'll keep bugging you for money until you just give in.

If you don't get outta that chair my finger's going in your asshole.
*Levanta dessa cadeira, senão **vou dar uma dedada no seu cu**.*

·····Chill out
Calma

If your wasted friend is talking shit to that guy who looks like he might be involved with *traficantes* (drug dealers), pair these kick-ass words with a nice brown smile.

Let it go.
Deixa disso.

Forget about it.
Deixa isso pra lá.

It's not worth it.
Não vale a pena.

Calm down, man.
Calma, rapaz.

Chill brah, there's nothing we can do about it.
Fica na sua broder, estamos de mãos atadas.

You're reading too much into it.
Tá vendo chifre em cabeça de cavalo.
Literally, "You're seeing horns on a horse's head."

You're seeing things.
Tá vendo cabelo em casca de ovo.
Literally, "You're seeing hair on an egg shell."

Get a hold of yourself!
Segura tua onda!

I made a mistake.
Dei um fora.

You're all worked up.
Você tá de cabeça quente.

Take it easy!
Pega leve!

Cool your jets!
Esfria a cabeça!

Take it down a notch.
Abaixa sua crista.
Literally, "Let down your rooster comb."

Simmer down.
Menos, Maria, menos.

Forget it, my brother.
Esquece isso, mermão.

Stay outta this.
Fica fora disso.

Take it outside.
Vai brigar lá fora.

Make love, not war.
Faça amor, não faça guerra.

I don't want to fight you.
Não quero brigar com você.

Let's have a beer and forget about this.
Vamos tomar uma cerveja e esquecer isso.

Let's be friends.
Vamos ser amigos.

CHAPTER 7

POPPY PORTUGUESE
PORTUGUÊS POPULAR

Brazil is a ginormous country with a giant mix of cultures. And like in the United States, the diversity you see in Brazil's society has been heavily influenced by its immigrants.

•••••Music
Música

Rihanna's R&B pop songs might be the shit in the U.S., but they sure ain't in Brazil. This part of the world grooves to its own unique musical sound that's heard everywhere: live in restaurants, blasted from parked cars, sung on the streets and especially played off people's cell phones and MP3 players.

To an outsider, Brazilian music is strictly samba, but there's MPB (*música popular brasileira*), *forró*, funk, rock, rap and a jillion other genres that don't fit into these categories. Pretty much every type of music also has it's own specific dance style, which is just as important as the music itself. There's no stiff Riverdance posture here—loosen up your hips and lose the inhibitions so you don't look like a complete fool when you bust out the dance moves.

Do you know where there's a...**concert?**
*Você sabe onde tem **show** do/a...?*
Note: *Show* is a rocking concert while *concerto* is something a little more lame, I mean tame, like an orchestra performance.

Do you like... ?
Você gosta de... ?

I hate...
Eu odeio...

I love...
Adoro...

How do you dance to... ?
Como se dança... ?

Samba

We say samba, you say Brazil (and Carnaval and feathered headdresses and women clad in sparkly, dental-floss "clothes"...). Originally a traditional dance among African slaves, the samba wasn't sexy (or widely known) until it got to Rio, where it transformed into what it is today—fast-paced and hot, with tons of variations distinguished by types of instruments used and lyrics performed. Want a more traditional samba? Look for *samba de roda* or *samba recôncavo*. Like to gawk at flashy costumes and fine (we mean, really fine) women? It's *samba carioca* for you. Got a soft spot for jazz stylings? Try *samba partido alto*. There's also *samba reggae*, *samba com rap* and *samba enredo*—a samba for all tastes is out there somewhere.

Popular artists: Beth Carvalho, Zeca Pagodinho (*carioca*); Fundo de Quintal, Revelação, Délcio Luis (*partido alto*); Olodum, Ilê Aye (*samba reggae*); Marcelo D2, Rappin Hood (*samba com rap*)

MPB

MPB (*música popular brasileira*) puts a modern spin on classic Brazilian sounds. It's easy-listening rock without the smaltzy connotation.

Popular artists: Caetano Veloso, Gilberto Gil, Vanessa da Mata, Marisa Monte.

Bossa Nova

Influenced by American jazz, Bossa Nova is slow and calm with mellow lyrics. This is samba on tranquilizers.

Popular artists: Tom Jobim, João Gilberto, Vinicius de Moraes

Pagode

What do you get when you mix sirens and cell phone rings with a jammin' rhythm and bad-ass lyrics? Basically, upbeat party music, or *pagode*. When the amps are full blast, expect to see lots of people dancing like they're dry humping the air.

Popular artists: Psirico, Parangole

Axé

Translated as "good energy," *axé* is shiny, happy percussion music best experienced live. The singers feed off the audience's energy and vice versa. You can't stand still for *axé*, and if you can't dance, just jump. If you're in Salvador for Carnaval, you'll definitely here *axé* music.

Popular artists: Ivete Sangalo, Timbalada, Chiclete com Banana

Forró

A cross between the freaking you did in middle school and square dancing, *forró* is like polka music with a Latin flair. You can't escape the sounds of *forró* during June in northeast Brazil, where it's the official music of the region's Festa Junina. In some cities it's even prohibited to play any other rhythm during this time. But the music isn't limited to June or the northeast—*forró* is loved year-round all over the country.

Popular artists: Luiz Gonzaga, Dominguinhos, Adelmario Coelho, Flávio José

Funk Carioca (Rio Funk)

A rhythm straight from the *favelas* of Rio, *funk carioca* is popular all over Brazil. Get your freak on, because this music is bumpin'.

Popular artists: Bochecha, MC Sapão

Other music styles you're likely to hear are *maracatu, sertanejo*, *repente*, *xoro*, *marchinhas de carnaval*, *arrocha*, pop-rock, rock, rap and reggae. We're sure you skipped over the long definitions above, so we're not even going to try with the rest of the music. If you're interested, just Wikipedia it.

Where can I hear live music?
*Onde tem **música ao vivo**?*

What's your favorite band?
Qual é a sua banda preferida?

> **Timbalada is my favorite band.**
> *Timbalada é a minha banda favorita.*

Did you see the YouTube video of Fundo de Quintal?
Você viu o vídeo do Fundo de Quintal no YouTube?

·····Bootlegs
Pirataria

The best thing about Brazil is that you can buy everything you need on the streets: fruit, meat, clothes, toothbrushes, sink plugs, oatmeal, sunglasses and, of course, bootlegs.

> **Do you have *Lethal Weapon 4*?**
> *Você tem Maquina Mortífera 4?*

> **Can I have three for ten *reais*?**
> *Você pode fazer três por dez?*

Is this in English?
É em inglês?

Does it have subtitles?
Tem legenda?

Because live music is such a big thing in Brazil, so are concert DVDs. You can find pirated versions of a live performance for just about any one of your favorite bands. From Michael Jackson to Jorge Ben Jor, from Akon to Caetano Veloso, they've got it all.

Do you have Ivete Sangalo's new DVD?
Você tem o novo DVD da Ivete Sangalo?

Can I check it out before I buy it?
Posso dar uma olhada antes de comprar?

·····Movies
Filmes

Most American movies in Brazil are dubbed, so make sure your movie is in English with Portuguese subtitles or be prepared to read lips. They are also given completely different names. If you want to see Naked Gun, look for it under its much catchier Brazilian title: *Corra Que a Polícia Vem Aí* (Run the Police Are Coming).

Let's see a/an...on the big screen.
Vamos assistir um/uma...na tela grande.

chick flick
filme meloso

cartoon
desenho animado

comedy
comédia

documentary
documentário

action
filme de ação

LOL))) RSRS

Sometimes shit's so funny you've gotta express it in random letters on a keyboard.

Hehe (cute)

Kkkkk (That's as funny as *hehe*, but I'm too lazy to type it.)

Rsrs (funny)

Hahaha (That's not funny... but it could be funny.)

Hihihi (I'm laughing at you.)

Huahuahua (That's actually funny.)

Jkljikljkljklkjljk (I'm rolling on the floor that's so funny.)

drama
drama

Is that new kung-fu flick out yet?
Já lançaram aquele novo filme de kung-fu?

Do you want salt on your popcorn?
*Você quer sal na sua **pipoca**?*

That guy sitting next to me stinks.
O homem de meu lado tá fedendo.

•••••TV
Televisão

If there's anything that comes close to soccer in popularity in Brazil, it's television. People watch hours and hours of TV every day. But don't expect the latest HBO series at your buddy's *lar* (home)—it's more often than not just plain, old-fashioned (yup, no cable, no satellite), bunny-ears TV with bad reception.

You can also probably find an American show or movie on Brazilian TV—they air a lot of the same programs (but dubbed, of course). Oh, and whatever show you thought you were going to watch on a day when there's a soccer game, forget it. All normal programming is interrupted to broadcast the national obsession. Did we mention soccer was popular in Brazil?

Lets see what's on Globo.
Vamos ver o que tá passando na Globo.
Globo is the largest TV network in Brazil.

Change the channel, dude.
Troca de canal, cara.

What movie's on Band?
Que filme tá passando na Band?
Band (Rede Bandeirantes) is a São Paulo–based TV network that shows a lot of dubbed American movies.

BRAZILIAN TV SHOWS

Soaps
Novelas
Soap operas have their following in the States, but it's nothing like in Latin America. Brazil itself has its own crop of addictive *novelas* that have been translated into other languages (including Russian!). While the U.S. soaps aren't exactly the pinnicale of subtlety, Brazil takes it to another level of cheese with superdramatic, backstabbing, life-or-death plotlines for every aspect of ordinary life. And the likelihood of someone getting pregnant by the end of the show is about 90 percent.

Domingão do Faustão
Domingão do Faustão has been on every Sunday for, like, forever. It's a variety show with games, talent showcases, celebrity interviews and live music. In a particularly telegenic society, the host, Fausto Corrêa da Silva, happens to be a pudgy guy whose schtick is to interrupt the person he's

interviewing and then talk most of the full three hours of the program. Expect to be annoyed yet morbidly fascinated.

Fantástico

This newsmagazine show is kind of like *60 Minutes*, but with hotter hosts and softer stories. It airs on Sunday evening when pretty much everyone is at home chillin'.

Malhação

Wondering how to ease the kids into the popular Brazilian grown-up *novelas*? Look no further—here's a soap about the angst of being a teenager (imagine *Saved by the Bell* without the yucks). To maximize the 'tweener audience, it airs right around when school gets out.

Hoje em dia

This weekday morning show mixes news and entertainment with an emphasis on the fluffy. There are others, but this is one of the bigger ones. The host sits around and does interviews or teaches you how to cook something, but mostly just talks a lot.

Big Brother Brasil

This contrived reality show (though what reality show isn't contrived) has a HUGE following in Brazil.

A Praça É Nossa

A Praça É Nossa is a comedy show that's been around for years. The host, Carlos Alberto, sits on a park bench and meets some of the most random and hilarious characters. Staged, of course—the bench is in a TV studio.

·····Phones
Telefones

If you're old enough, you might remember a time in America when people were confined to using a landline telephone. Well, due to the high cost of cell phone plans and prepaid cards in Brazil, people still use those ancient public landlines called pay phones. You use your cell for a video camera or to listen to music, of course!

Landline phone
Telefone fixo

Cell phone
Celular

How do you turn the volume up on this **cell phone**?
*Como você aumenta o volume nesse **celular**?*

Prepaid phone card
Cartão telefônico

You can **call** me, I'll be awake.
*Pode **ligar** hoje, vou estar acordado.*

Where's the nearest **pay phone**?
*Onde tem um **orelhão** perto daqui?*
Orelhão literally means "big ear" and it looks like one, too— pretty clever, huh?

Can I use your computer to **download** a song to my phone?
*Eu posso usar o seu computador pra **baixar** uma música pro meu celular?*
It's not that common to have Internet access on your cell, so if you want to add a song to your phone's playlist, it's gotta be done through a computer.

·····Computers
Computadores

You may not think of Brazil as a wired society, but you'd be wrong. The largest country in South America ranks fifth in Internet usage worldwide (only behind China, the U.S., Japan and India).

> **Which Internet café do you go to?**
> *Qual **Lan house** que você frequenta?*

> **How much is it for 20 minutes?**
> *Quanto custa por vinte minutos?*

> **Do you have Skype?**
> *Você tem Skype?*

> **This headset is broken.**
> *Esse **fone** tá quebrado.*

> **Can I print something out?**
> *Posso **imprimir** uma coisa?*

> **Do you have a scanner?**
> *Tem um **scanner**?*

> **Can I make a copy of my ass?**
> *Posso **xerocar** a minha bunda?*

·····PC talk
Falar de computador

This may be the easiest Portuguese you learn—a lot of these words are just English pronounced with a Brazilian accent.

> **Website**
> *Site*

> > **Did you check out that porn website with the monkeys?**
> > *Já viu o **site** pornô com os macacos?*

Download
Download

> **I'm trying to download this zombie game.**
> *Tô tentando fazer download desse jogo de zumbís.*

Virus
Vírus

Hacker
Hacker

Flat screen
Monitor de LCD

Keyboard
Teclado

> **This keyboard is so weird.**
> *Esse teclado é tão esquisito.*

·····Social networking
Rede social

The most popular social networking sites in Brazil are Orkut and MSN, but don't fear, FB addicts—more and more people are using Facebook.

User name
Login

Password
Senha

> **What's your password?**
> *Qual é a sua senha?*

Profile
Perfil

Wall (Facebook)
Mural

> **You didn't even write on her wall.**
> *Você nem escreveu no mural dela.*

Wall (Orkut)
Página de recados

Message
Recado

Message (Orkut)
Scrap

> I sent you a **message** last week.
> *Eu mandei um **scrap** pra você na semana passada.*

Group
Communidade

Chat
Bate-papo

Blog
Blog

Post
Postar

> Nice jiggly ass in that pic you **posted** yesterday.
> *Gostei daquela foto com a bunda caída que você **postou**.*

E-mail
Email

To add
Adicionar

> I **added** you as a friend on Facebook.
> *Eu te **adicionei** no Facebook.*

To delete
Apagar

> You better **delete** your profile, your girlfriend's crazy mad.
> *Melhor **apagar** esse perfil, sua namorada tá pau da vida. (RJ)*

·····Text talk
Conversa escrita

Texting isn't that popular in Brazil, but MSN instant messaging sure as shit is.

Text...	Short for	English
K	*Que*	What
Pq	*Porque*	Why/because
Vc	*Você*	You
To	*Estou*	I am
Ta	*Está*	He/she is; you are
Tbm	*Também*	Also
Msm	*Mesmo*	Same/really
Blz	*Beleza*	Beauty/sweet!
9Dade	*Novidade*	News
V6	*Vocês*	You (plural)
Cmg	*Comigo*	With me
Td	*Tudo*	Everything
Dzer	*Dizer*	To say
Eh	*É*	Is
Naum	*Não*	No

CHAPTER 8

SPORTY PORTUGUESE
PORTUGUÊS ESPORTIVO

•••••Soccer
Futebol

You've gotta admit, one of the first things you think about when you hear the word "Brazil" is soccer. You're not the only one—everything in the country revolves around this glorious game. Every kid dreams about being a soccer player; every adult wants his son to be one; and every grandparent is disappointed that their son wasn't one. On the beach, on the grass, in the street, in the park, you'll see kids playing soccer everywhere. It's in their blood, it's in the curve of their feet and it's all over the place.

What's your favorite… ?
Qual é seu…favorito ?

That…is a corpse.
Esse…é uma carniça.

That…is so weak.
Esse…é uma mãe.

I like that… —that fool is good.
Gosto desse… —o sacana é bom.

> **team**
> *time*
>
> **franchise**
> *clube*
>
> **forward**
> *atacante*
>
> **midfielder**
> *meio campo*
>
> **sweeper**
> *lateral*
>
> **defender**
> *zagueiro*
>
> **goalie**
> *goleiro*
>
> **coach**
> *técnico*
>
> **ref**
> *juiz*
>
> **linesman**
> *banderinha*
> Literally, "little flag."

For those of you who actually wanna play instead of yelling at the ref or waving your shirt around your head, here are some things you might want to know how to say:

> **Let's go play a pickup game with our college buddies.**
> *Vamos pegar **uma pelada** com os colegas da faculdade.* (RJ) | *…**um baba**…* (BA)
>
> **Nice goal!**
> *Golaço!*
>
> **Nutmeg**
> *Caneta*
> Passing the ball through the defender's legs.

Chip pass
Chapéu
Passing the ball over a defender's head.

Pass to yourself
Meia lua
Literally, "half moon." This move is like a through pass to oneself; a player kicks the ball to the side of the defender then runs around behind the defender to get the pass.

Quick pass
Tabela

Header
Cabeçada

Dribble
Conduzir
Literally, "drive."

Hey! I'm open, kick it here!
Aqui! Tô sózinho, passa pra mim!

Bad fucking pass!
Bola filha da puta!

That wasn't a foul!
Você inventou essa falta!
Literally, "You invented this foul."

·····At the stadium
No estádio

The first thing you need to know about soccer stadiums is that they, too, have nicknames. No venue is referred to by the official name written in huge letters above the main entrance, so don't get confused when you arrive at what your friends call the *Maracanã* and the sign says Mario Filho Stadium—it's the same place. The second thing you need to know is that the stadium is like a crazy house. It's the only place (besides a crazy house) where someone can shout, cry, fight and sometimes get hit by a flying bag of piss without a passing glance.

What time's the game?
Que horas é o jogo?

Who are you rooting for?
Para quem você torce?

My team's gonna...
Meu time vai...

> **dominate.**
> *dar uma lavada.*
>
> **score a ton of goals.**
> *dar uma goleada.*
>
> **humiliate the other team.**
> *dar um chocolate.*
> Kind of like the sweet taste of victory.
>
> **fuck some shit up!**
> *botar pra fuder!*

RiVALRiES)))
RIVALIDADES

Most rivalries are between clubs within the same city, making these urban match-ups the fiercest and most exciting. The matches are so important to the fans that they even warrant their own melded nicknames (basically the team names shortened and squished together). So when Flamengo and Fluminese (RJ) play, it's the FlaFlu game; when Bahia and Vitória (BA) meet, it's BaVi; when Santos and São Paulo (SP) play, it's SanSão; and so on.

But none of these rivalries compare to the sheer hatred between Brazil and Argentina. If you dare to say *"Maradona foi melhor do que Pelé"* ("Maradona was better than Pelé"; that would be Argentine soccer great Diego Maradona and Brazilian legend Pelé), you might suddenly find yourself crying on the floor, begging for your life. By the way, Pelé was the best.

That foul wasn't a red card! This fucking ref is making bad calls.
Essa falta não foi pra cartão vermelho! Esse juiz desgraçado tá roubando!

That guy's a star player.
Esse muleque é craque.

This team's fans suffer.
Torcedor desse time sofre.

Aww, come on!
Haaa, qualé?

Goal's wide open—shoot it!
Chuta que o gol tá aberto!

Can you bring me a beer at half time?
Você pode me trazer uma cerveja no intervalo?
Don't think you'll be saying this at the stadium, unless you want non-alcoholic beer. That's right—no alcoholic beverages or glass bottles.

·····Other sports
Outros esportes

Suprisingly, there are other sports in Brazil besides soccer. Of course there's no comparison, but there's gotta be something to do for the people with two left feet.

Indoor soccer
Futsal / Futebol de Salão

Volleyball
Vôlei

Handball
Handebol

Basketball
Basquete

Tennis
Tênis

Swimming
Natação

Gymnastics
Ginástica

•••••At the beach
Na praia

There's so much going on at the beach already, but for those with ADD, there are plenty of games and sports that are only played there.

Beach soccer
Futebol de areia
This is basically soccer, but with fewer players, a shorter play time, a smaller area, and you play on the sand.

Beach volleyball
Vôlei de praia / Futvolei
Brazilians love soccer so much they've created this game—it's volleyball, but you can't use your hands. You see this all over the beaches in Rio.

Rugby
Rugby

Badmiton
Peteca
For the old folks on Sunday morning.

Paddle ball
Frescobol

Scuba diving
Mergulho

Surfing
Surf

Windsurfing
Windsurf

Boogieboarding
Bodyboard

Kitesurfing
Kitesurfe

The waves are big today.
O mar tá gigante hoje.
Mar is literally "ocean."

Can I rent a board here?
Posso alugar uma prancha aqui?

This guy doesn't know how to surf for shit.
Esse cara é o maior raule.

Did you wax my board?
Você passou parafina na minha prancha?

·····Martial arts
Artes marcias

Capoeira
Developed by slaves in colonial Brazil, this unique Brazilian martial art is rooted deep in the country's cultural identity. *Capoeira* is a mix of fight, dance and acrobatics set to music. Whether seen as dancing or fighting, *capoeira* is kickass! Call it what you will (one friend says it's "hippy-dance-fighting"), when it comes down to it, those high-flying kicks and quick takedowns are serious business. *Capoeira* is big countrywide, but in Bahia, it's so much a part of the every day life that you'll see it on the streets, hear the music in shops and observe people practicing it on the beach.

Jiu-jitsu
Brazilian jiu-jitsu is a full-on contact sport that evolved from Japanese judo. This extremely popular self-defense discipline is known for its demobilizing grappling techniques, so if a jiu-jitsu master gets you on the ground, you're fucked.

Mixed Martial Arts
MMA
Somebody somewhere thought it would be cool to see which martial art was the most bad-ass and created this now very popular genre.

Boxing
Boxe
Boxing is at all the gyms, but it's not as popular as the other martial arts. It's a great way to lose calories, which is why there are so many girl boxers in Brazil.

Muay Thai
Think of a guy whose punches are as quick as a boxer's, whose kicks are as strong as a *capoeirista*'s and who really wants to hurt you. Muay thai is spreading all over Brazil.

Judo
Judô
You need money to practice *judô*. It's like the golf of Brazilian martial arts.

·····Working out
Malhação

In Brazil, the gym is a place that's open to everyone of all shapes and sizes. Yeah right. Don't even think about going there with your old high school P.E. shirt and a ratty pair of tennis shoes. The gym is full of good-looking people; and for those who aren't pretty, they certainly are wearing some styling new kicks and a matching outfit to make up for it.

Where is/are…?
Onde fica…?

the gym
a academia

the freeweights
as nilhas

bench press
o supino

> **I bench 10 pounds**—I'm gonna get strong quickly.
> ***Eu pego 5 quilos no supino***—*vou ficar forte rápido.*

the treadmill
a esteira

excercise bike
a bicicleta

the pool
a piscina

How many push-ups can you do?
*Quantos **flexões** você pode fazer? | ...**apoios**...? (BA)*

Dude, I've seen harder pillows than your stomach. You need to do some sit-ups.
*Rapaz, eu já vi travesseiros mais duros que o seu abdomen. Você precisa fazer **abdominal**.*

I need to stretch.
*Preciso **alongar**.*

I **go jogging** every morning.
*Eu **corro** toda manhã.*

What time is the **yoga** class?
*A que horas é a aula de **yoga**?*

We should do the **Bahian swing** class together.
*Devemos fazer a aula de **swing baiano** juntos.*

I've gotta start **working out** because it's almost summer.
*Preciso começar a **malhar** porque o verão tá chegando.*

How long have you been **lifting**?
*Há quanto tempo você faz **musculação**?*

You're never gonna get strong using **dog steroids**.
*Você nunca vai ficar forte tomando **esteróides pra cachorro**.*

This gym didn't have that many **machines**. I didn't like it.
*Essa academia tem poucos **aparelhos**. Não gostei.*

·····Sports clubs
Clubes

The sports clubs in Brazil are like Disneyland for exercise nuts. Besides the gym, pool, tennis courts, soccer fields, basketball and volleyball courts, they have various restaurants and a large concert space where some of the country's most popular artists perform. Some clubs are specific to a single sport (yacht clubs, tennis clubs) but most have everything you need to have a comfortable sporting day. It's the best place to hang out on the weekends and during summer.

I want to become a **member**.
*Quero ser **sócio**.*

The **monthly fee** here is ridiculously expensive.
*A **mensalidade** é cara pra caralho.*

Can I bring a guest?
*Posso trazer um **convidado**?*

My membership card expires tomorrow.
*Minha **carteira de sócio** vence amanhã.*

•••••Games
Jogos

Pool
Sinuca

Bowling
Boliche

Foosball
Totó

Futebol do botão
It's a cross between checkers and foosball, and it's really fun.

Cards
Baralho

Dominoes
Dominó

Ping-pong
Ping-pong
Don't forget, that's pronounced *pingy pongy*.

Chess
Xadrez

•••••Video games
Vídeo games

Vídeo games are universal. Created in Japan, named in the U.S. and played worldwide, video games are beautiful because they're the same in every language (or they're just the same language and pronounced differently).

Do you know how to play… ?
Você sabe jogar… ?

Do you have… ?
Você tem… ?

Are you good at… ?
Você é bom de… ?

> **PlayStation**
> *Play station (play stay-CHION)*
>
> **Xbox**
> *Xbox (sheez-box)*
>
> **Nintendo Wii**
> *Nintendo Wii*
>
> **Atari**
> *Atari*
>
> **Nintendo 64**
> *Nintendo 64 (Nintendo meia-quatro)*
>
> **007**
> *007 (zero zero sete)*
>
> **Winning Eleven**
> *Winning Eleven (Wingy-Eleven)*
>
> **Pro Evolution Soccer**
> *PES*

Should we play against each other or together?
Vamos jogar contra ou cooperativo?

Bring over your controller because mine's broken.
Traz o seu controle porque meu tá quebrado.

CHAPTER 9

HUNGRY PORTUGUESE
PORTUGUÊS COM FOME

If you're jonesin' for some eats in Brazil, you won't be for long—there are food stands and restaurants everywhere. But don't expect a bland plate of beige grub—like the people, Brazilian food is full of color, flavor and spice. And though it's easy to score some food fast, it won't be fast food—no walking and eating here. Wanna blend in with the local diners? Then sit down, relax and savor your tasty treat.

•••••Hunger
Fome

You hungry?
Tá com fome?

Hell yeah, I'm hungry.
Tô com uma fome danada.

I'm starving.
Tô caindo de fome.

I'm dying of hunger.
Tô morrendo de fome.

I'm so famished I could eat a horse.
Tô com tanta fome, que seria capaz de comer um boi.
Boi is literally "bull."

I'm so hungry I'm about to pass out.
Tô desmaiando de fome.

I'm jonesing for some…food.
Tô a fim de uma comida…

American
americana
Don't ask for "American" food—nobody will know what you're talking about. Just ask where the nearest *lanchonete* (café) is. This is where you'll find cheeseburgers (*x-burgers*, pronounced "sheez-burger"), milkshakes (*milkshakes*) and fries (*batata fritas*). Other typical sandwich offerings: the americano with ham, cheese, egg, lettuce, tomato and mayo; the hamburger, like an American burger but also made with bacon, ham and eggs…the way a hamburger should be; and the *frango na chapa*, grilled chicken and ham.

Chinese
chinesa
Chinese food has been adapted to the South American palate, so a spring roll in Brazil is filled with cheese instead of vegetables. Yup, cheese, a food that's never used in real Chinese cooking. But hey, if you're into that, go ahead.

Italian
italiana
At least Brazilians got something somewhat right. Pasta and pizza—delish!

There's not enough ketchup in this **pasta**.
*Não tem ketchup suficiente nesse **macarrão**.*
Wondering why the bottles of ketchup and mustard are on the table? Brazilians like to put it on their pizza or in their pasta. You can skip it if you want.

Japanese
japonesa
São Paulo is chockfull of Japanese-Brazilians who've managed to keep their food authentic. It's popular all over the country.

Mexican
mexicana
Yeah…the tortillas don't quite cut it. But why eat Mexican when in Brazil?

Middle Eastern
árabe
You'll mostly find Middle-Eastern food served in fast-food joints: Armenian pizza (their version of *lahmajoon*), *kibe* (made with beef instead of lamb), tabbouleh and hummus.

I'm not hungry—I just scarfed down some *coxinhas*.
*Estou sem fome—acabei de devorar umas **coxinhas**.*

No, I just ate dinner.
Não, acabei de jantar.

I'm OK, I just had a huge lunch.
Tô bem. Comi um almoço enorme.

I've got the munchies.
Tô com larica.

Let's eat.
Vamos rangar.

Should we eat at that new Japanese joint?
Vamos comer naquele boteco Japones novo?

Did you have breakfast already?
Você já tomou café?

Do you want to have dinner with me tonight?
Você quer jantar comigo hoje à noite?

Let's grab a bite to eat before we hit the club.
Vamos fazer um lanche antes de ir pra boate.

·····Eating out
Comer fora

Lunch is the heaviest meal in Brazil, which means that for many, eating out happens at midday rather than in the evening. There's an infinite number of dining options to satisfy those cravings.

Let's go to...
Vamos pra...

a restaurant.
um restaurante.

an all-you-can-eat place.
um rodízio.
This isn't the pork-out buffets you see all over the U.S.— *rodízio*-style dining means servers come around with trayfuls of food until you've hit your limit. Usually *rodízios* serve pizza and pasta or seafood and steak.

a café.
uma lanchonete.
A café is a great place to grab a quick bite when you're out and about. The menu usually has fresh juice, *açai na tigela* (frozen açai berries blended into a thick paste and sprinkled with granola or other fruit like bananas), ham-and-cheese sandwiches and baked treats.

a café. (in the cute French sense)
um café.
These exist for tourists, but you won't see too many people drinking tall lattes or iced Frappuccinos. Caffeine is usually plain old coffee and maybe espresso. But honestly, real Brazilians get their coffee fix at *lanchonetes* (where it's served in small plastic cups) or from old men selling the brew from street carts.

a steakhouse.
uma churrascaria.
The glorious *churrascaria* is like a good ol' Texas steakhouse with meat, meat and meat on the menu. There's also the *rodízio*-style *churrascaria*, where servers come around with giant skewered hunks of grilled beef and carve pieces for you tableside. A giant buffet in the middle of the restaurant is filled

with all-you-can-eat, rice, beans, salads and sometimes sushi. When you've stuffed your face too much, flip over that little green card on your table to the red side so the server stops bringing you meat and comes over with the dessert tray.

a fast-food restaurant.
um restaurante fast-food.
McDonald's is a delicacy here.

food-by-the-kilo restaurant
restaurante de comida a kilo.
These buffet-style restaurants are like supermarket salad bars but with entrées and side dishes thrown in. You pay by the kilo (usually 15 to 25 *reais* per kilo). Get as much as you want, but remember, it's all on your dime. Don't lose your receipt, because the cost of a lost ticket is enough food to feed an elephant.

lunch plate
prato feito / PF
At most *comida a kilo* restaurants they offer a fixed-price plate that's usually your choice of meat with rice, beans and salad. If you're hungry and want a lot of food for a good price, this is the way to go; it's generally cheaper than if you were to weigh the same plate of food.

Menu
Cardápio

Order
Pedido

> **Has the waiter taken your order?**
> *O moço já anotou o seu **pedido**?*

Expensive
Caro

Cheap
Barato

Tip
Gorjeta

> **I'm broke, I can't leave a tip.**
> *Tô duro, não posso **dar gorjeta.***
> Your server doesn't expect a tip—it's totally optional.

Bon appétit!
Bom apetite!

•••••Yum!!!
Hummmm!!!!

Everyone likes compliments, especially cooks, so if you like a dish, be vocal about it.

> **Delicious.**
> *Delicioso.*

> **Scrumptious.**
> *Gostoso.*

> **Delish.**
> *Uma delícia.*

> **I want more.**
> *Quero mais.*

> **Just a little bit more.**
> *Só mais um pouquinho.*

Loved it!
Amei!

I'm satisfied.
Tô satisfeito.
It's more polite to use this expression when declining food rather than *Tô cheio* (I'm full); saying you're full can be considered rude.

After I ate that *feijoada*, I had a food coma.
*Despois de comer essa **feijoada**, eu **apagei**.*

·····Nasty
Desagradável

As adventurous as you think you are with food, there's gonna be something that'll churn your stomach.

Your beans taste burned.
Seu feijão tá com gosto de queimado.

That food's disgusting—I can't even swallow it!
Esse rango tá nojento—Não desce!

Jesus, are you going to eat that? Gross!
*Meu Deus, você vai comer isso? **Que nojo!***

Yuck!
Argh!

The food was...
A comida tava...

>**spoiled.**
>*estragada.*
>
>**crap.**
>*uma porcaria.*
>
>**awful.**
>*ruim.*
>
>**too sweet.**
>*muito doce.*
>
>**too salty.**
>*muito salgada.*

too sour.
muito azeda.

•••••Drinks
Bebidas

It's gonna be hot and you're gonna get thirsty. Fainting does not make you attractive. Stay hydrated!

I'm...
Tô ...

thirsty.
com sede.

parched.
morto de sede.

dehydrated.
desidratado.

Can I have a glass of water?
Eu quero um copo d'água.
It may seem rude, but when you're asking for something, you usually just say "I want" instead of "Can I have?"

My girlfriend only drinks sparkling water, but I prefer still.
*Minha namorada só bebe **água com gás**, mas eu prefiro água **sem gás**.*

Tap
Da torneira

I got the runs for a week after I drank tap water.
*Tive diarréia por uma semana depois que tomei água **da torneira**.*

Don't give me room-temp water—I want it nice and cold.
*Não me de água **natural**—eu quero bem gelada.*

Coconut water's the jam!
***Água de coco** é legal!*

Best when fresh out of a green coconut—usually how it's served on the beach, on the street or at a *lanchonete*. But you can also buy this tropical treat in stores (bottled or boxed). Oh, and careful with the pronunciation: "CO-co" (accent on the first syllable) means "coconut"; "co-CÔ" (accent on the last syllable) means "shit." I mean, unless you want shitty water.

Sugarcane
Caldo de cana

I want…juice.
Quero suco de…

> **guava**
> *goiaba*

> **lime**
> *limão*

> **mango**
> *manga*

> **orange**
> *laranja*

> **passion fruit**
> *maracujá*

> **pineapple**
> *abacaxí*

Avocado smoothie
Vitamina de abacate

An avocado smoothie may sound weird, but don't dis it till you've tried it. Mixed with milk and sugar, this super-popular choice plays to the avocado's true nature (it is, after all, a fruit). If you aren't adventurous, you can opt for a smoothie from more familiar additions like bananas (*bananas*) or papayas (*mamões*). Boring.

Frappe
Batida

Coffee
Café

> **black**
> *preto*

decaf
descaifeinado

with or without...?
com ou sem...?

> **milk**
> *leite*

> **sugar**
> *açúcar*

> **sweetener**
> *adoçante*

Cup of coffee
Xícara de café

Small coffee
Cafezinho

Tea
Chá

Soda
Refrigerante
Brazil's favorite soft drink is *guaraná*, and Guaraná Antártica is the most popular brand.

> **regular**
> *normal*

> **diet**
> *zero / light / diet*

·····Traditional Brazilian dishes
Pratos brasileiros tradicionais

Lip-smacking, melt-in-your-mouth food—that's Brazilian cuisine. Hope you like beans and rice (*feijão com arroz*) because that, along with the occasional salad (*salada*), comes with just about every meal. There are tons of options and you should try them all. Here are a few suggestions.

Feijoada
A salted-pork and black bean stew served with rice…and other things.

LOCAL FRUITS)))
FRUTAS LOCAIS

Some tropical fruits never make it north of the equator. If you see something at the market or on the menu you've never tasted before, don't be a sissy—try it. Brazilians have been enjoying these delectables for ages, so it won't kill you, and you may even fall in love with it.

Siriguela: This is similar in look and flavor to a kumquat.

Cupuaçu: Related to the *cacao* fruit, *cupuaçu* is usually served in juice form.

Graviola: Soursops have a spiny exterior; the custardy flesh is tart.

Jaca: The jackfruit is not as stinky as a durian but it certainly is pungent.

Umbú: This small Brazilian plum is green and tart.

Acerola: The Barbados or West Indian cherry isn't native to Brazil but thrives in the climate. Another tart fruit that's super high in vitamin C.

Açaí: A berry a little smaller than a blueberry. This fruit is known as a natural energy booster. You'll see it as ice cream, juice, blended with other fruit then topped with tapioca or granola.

Moqueca

Seafood stew. *Moqueca capixaba*, influenced by Native Brazilian cuisine, is cooked in a traditional clay pot and can be made with fish, shrimp, crab or lobsters. In the northeast, *moqueca baiana* takes on African touches with the addition of coconut milk and palm oil (*dendê*), which gives this stew a distinctive yellow tint. Served with *farinha* (manioc flour), rice, salad and sometimes black-eyed peas.

Tutú à mineira

A paste of beans and manioc flour. Very popular in Minas Gerais.

Vaca atolada

Literally, "mud-stranded cow." Sounds a little gross, but it's a popular meat and cassava stew typical of *caipira* cuisine from the interior of the state of São Paulo.

Arroz carreteiro

Typical of Rio Grande do Sul, this rice dish is mixed with meat and spices.

Bobó de camarão

This northeastern dish is made with a cooked cassava paste, palm oil, spices and shrimp.

Escondidinho

The name of this dish means "hidden," which refers to the *carne de sol* (salty dry beef) that's hidden beneath a layer of cassava purée and served with lots of *pimenta* (hot sauce).

Feijão tropeiro

Pinto beans mixed with manioc flour, sausage, bacon, eggs, onions and spices. It is served with meat and rice.

Empadão goiano

This is the chicken potpie of Goias, a state in central Brazil; it can also be made with sausage or corn.

Bacalhau

Salted codfish. *Bacalhau* is very popular in Brazil because of the whole Portuguese influence. It's cooked many ways, but the most common preparation is baked with various spices.

·····Street food
Comida na rua

You'll never go hungry in Brazil—every other inch of dirt or pavement sports a food cart. But don't expect diet-conscious preparations—just enjoy the oh-so-yummy fat.

Acarajé (BA)

Peeled black-eyed peas formed into a ball and deep-fried in palm oil, then split in half and stuffed with *vatapá* (spicy peanut, shrimp and palm oil paste), *carurú* (a cooked okra mush) and tomato salad.

Bolinhos de chuvas

Everyone has their version of sweet fried dough. This is Brazil's.

Bolinhos de bacalhau
Salt-cod fritters.

Cocada
Sugar-coated grated coconut. *Cocada queimada* (or *cocada puxa-puxa*) is a chewier version made with brown sugar. *Cocada branca* is made with condensed milk, so it's whiteish instead of brownish.

Coxinha
Similar to a chicken croquette, but the shape resembles a chicken drumstick. The name literally means "little thigh."

Cachorro quente
Hot dog. Go tame and top with ketchup and mustard, or go local and add peas, corn, fried shoestring potatoes and tomato sauce.

Churrasco de gato
Meat on a stick; literally, "cat barbecue." The meat on the cart might look sketchy, but it's fine. And it's not cat meat, like hot dogs aren't dog meat. That's just the name.

Empadinha
Mini potpie filled with shrimp, chicken or beef.

Kibe
Kibbeh, a savory deep-fried combination of wheat, beef (instead of the usual lamb), mint and peanuts.

Mingau
Sweet breakfast porridge made with tapioca, corn or oatmeal.

Milho cozido
Corn on the cob. If you want salt and butter, order *com sal e manteiga*.

Pamonha
A paste made from corn and milk that's boiled and wrapped in corn husks. It can be salty or sweet, and can be filled with cheese, sausage or peppers.

Pão de queijo
Baked cheese balls.

Pastel

A crisp, fried pastry filled with sweet (*doce*) or savory (*salgado*) ingredients like guava jelly and cheese, banana, chocolate, coconut, meat and cheese.

Pipoca

Popcorn comes either salted (*salgada*) or sweet (*doce*).

Beijú

Made with tapioca starch, this tortillalike, flat cake is folded over and filled with the same kinds of stuff you see in *pastéis*.

•••••Beach food
Comida na praia

You don't bring a lot of shit to the beach. That's what dorky *farofeiros* (people who lug the kitchen sink to the beach) do. Definitely not cool. No, Brazilian beaches are full of people selling ice cream, popsicles, grilled shrimp, meat, fried fish, beer, water, soda and pretty much anything you'd like (or wouldn't like) to eat or drink.

Shrimp
Camarão

Kebab
Espetinho

Popsicle
Picolé

Crab broth
Caldo de sururú (BA)
Nice and hot, brought to you in some dude's thermos!

Fish
Peixe
Usually served fried (*frito*), but you can ask for it grilled (*grelhado*).

Just beer won't do, we need some salty snacks.
*Só cerveja não dá, precisa ter **tira-gosto**.*

Sandwich
Sanduíche

You're not gonna find a BLT or club on any menu—there's nothing too fancy here. The most common is *misto* (ham and cheese) or *natural* (chicken, lettuce and carrots). They can be toasted (*quente*) or cold (*frio*).

Queijo coalho

Salty, lightweight cheese browned over a hand-held charcoal oven, often sprinkled with oregano and/or garlic, and sometimes eaten with molasses.

Cashews
Castanhas

These come sweet, salty, natural or spicy and go great with a *brisa* (beer).

Oysters
Lambretas

On a half shell, served with lime and hot sauce.

·····Sweets
Doces

Always leave room for dessert. Can you say "delicious"?

Candy
Doce

Brigadeiro
Sort of like a truffle, this candy is made with chocolate, condensed milk, butter and cocoa powder, then topped with sprinkles.

Beijinho
Like *brigadeiro*, but made with coconut instead of chocolate.

Romeo e Julieta
Slices of *queijo de Minas* (soft, mild white cheese) and *goiabada* (guava paste) eaten together.

Cake
Bolo
Cake is what's for breakfast in Brazil. It's not the gooey, frosting-coated type, but it's got a wide variety of flavors. Some of the more unique ones are *fubá* (a type of corn), *aimpim* (yucca), *tapioca* (tapioca) and *banana* (banana).

Tart/Cake
Torta
This is any sort of elaborate cake with frosting or layers. It can also be a tart.

Mousse
Mousse
Mousses come in various fruit flavors, but the *mousse de maracujá* (passion fruit mousse) is the bomb diggity.

Coconut custard
Quindim
A gelatinous treat made with eggs, sugar and grated coconut.

Cookie
Biscoito

In every supermarket, corner store or gas station there is a wall full of cookies. They range from wafers to Oreo-sandwich–style to shortbread.

Ice cream
Sorvete

Peanut brittle
Pé de moleque

Trifle
Pavê

Flan
Pudim

·····Other Ulysses Press Titles

Dirty Chinese: Everyday Slang from "What's Up?" to "F*%# Off!"

MATT COLEMAN & EDMUND BACKHOUSE, **$10.00**

Dirty Chinese includes phrases for every situation, even expressions to convince a local official that you have waited long enough and tipped him plenty already. A pronunciation guide, a reference dictionary and sample dialogues make this guide invaluable for those traveling to China.

Dirty French: Everyday Slang from "What's Up?" to "F*%# Off!"

ADRIEN CLAUTRIER & HENRY ROWE, **$10.00**

With this book, you can use sweet words to entice a local beauty into a walk along the Seine, and less-than-philosophical rebuffs for those zealous, espresso-fueled cafe "poets." There are enough insults and swear words to offend every person in France without even speaking to them in English.

Dirty German: Everyday Slang from "What's Up?" to "F*%# Off!"

DANIEL CHAFFEY, **$10.00**

Dirty German provides plenty of insults and swear words to piss off every person in Germany—without even mentioning that the Japanese make better cars —as well as explicit sex terms that'll even embarrass the women of Hamburg's infamous red light district.

Dirty Italian: Everyday Slang from "What's Up?" to "F*%# Off!"

GABRIELLE EUVINO, **$10.00**

This useful guide contains phrases for every situation, including insults to hurl at the refs during *fútbol* games.

Readers learn sweet words to entice a local beauty into a romantic gondola ride, not-so-sweet remarks to ward off any overzealous Venetians, and more.

Dirty Japanese: Everyday Slang from "What's Up?" to "F*%# Off!"

MATT FARGO, **$10.00**

Even in traditionally minded Japan, slang from its edgy pop culture constantly enter into common usage. This book fills in the gap between how people really talk in Japan and what Japanese language students are taught.

Dirty Russian: Everyday Slang from "What's Up?" to "F*%# Off!"

ERIN COYNE & IGOR FISUN, **$10.00**

An invaluable guide for off-the-beaten-path travelers going to Russia, *Dirty Russian* is packed with enough insults and swear words to offend every person in Russia without even mentioning that they lost the Cold War.

Dirty Spanish: Everyday Slang from "What's Up?" to "F*%# Off!"

JUAN CABALLERO & NICK DENTON-BROWN, **$10.00**

This handbook features slang for both Spain and Latin America. It includes a section on native banter that will help readers make friends over a pitcher of sangría and convince the local taco maker that it's OK to spice things up with a few fresh habaneros.

To order these books call 800-377-2542 or 510-601-8301, fax 510-601-8307, e-mail ulysses@ulyssespress.com, or write to Ulysses Press, P.O. Box 3440, Berkeley, CA 94703. All retail orders are shipped free of charge. California residents must include sales tax. Allow two to three weeks for delivery.

•••••About the Authors

Alice Rose graduated with a BA in literature and a fetish for Brazilian culture. She lived in Brazil, where she learned how to be Brazilian—she is now late for almost everything. When she is not trying to learn how to samba, or working on her Bahian accent, she is digging up dinosaur bones in her backyard in Oakland, California.

Nati Vale is a native Puerto Rican with a Bahian swing in her step. She gets a kick out of pretending she's Brazilian, especially in Portugal. Though she'll never admit to it, she loves talking dirty. She currently lives in Berkeley, California, where she's attempting to finish her dissertation one paragraph at a time.

Pedro A. Cabral discovered Brazil in 1500. He spent most of his life in Salvador, Brazil. Due to GPS technology and Google Maps, Cabral has been forced to give up his love for exploration and has retired to tame Oakland, California, where he has dedicated himself to the art of capoeira.